CULTURES OF THE WORLD

Malaysia

WITHDRAWN

Marshall Cavendish
Benchmark
New York

PICTURE CREDITS

Cover: © Wendy Chan/Getty Images
Anders Blomqvist/Lonely Planet Images: 3, 12, 18, 55 • Christer Fredriksson/Lonely Planet Images: 41 • Danita Delimont/Getty Images: 66 • Eightfish/Getty Images: 128 • Felix Hug/Lonely Planet Images: 98 • Fred Ramage/ Getty Images: 26 • Goh Seng Chong/Bloomberg/Getty Images: 92, 118 • Greg Elms/Lonely Planet Images: 126 • Hoang Dinh Nam/AFP/Getty Images: 108 • Inmagine: 5, 11, 14, 16, 17, 20, 21, 22, 23, 28, 30, 46, 50, 68, 69, 76, 77, 78, 94, 95, 100, 102, 109, 116, 117, 124 • John Sones/Lonely Planet Images: 86 • Kevin Levesque/ Lonely Planet Images: 72 • Lawrence Bartlett/AFP/Getty Images: 84 • Marshall Cavendish International (Asia): 135 • Peter Ptschelinzew/Lonely Planet Images: 89 • Peter Solness/Lonely Planet Images: 63, 99, 104 • Philip Game/Lonely Planet Images: 1 • photolibrary: 6, 8, 9, 10, 13, 15, 34, 36, 38, 39, 56, 58, 60, 64, 74, 91, 97, 107, 112, 113, 120, 131 • Richard I'Anson/Lonely Planet Images: 79 • Richard Nebesky/Lonely Planet Images: 7 • Ron Sachs-Pool/Getty Images: 31 • Roslan Rahman/AFP/Getty Images: 32 • Saeed Khan/AFP/Getty Images: 33 • Stanley Chou/Getty Images: 110 • Tom Cockrem/Lonely Planet Images: 52 • Yellow Street Photos/Lonely Planet Images: 44

PRECEDING PAGE

Two young Malay school girls in the Kampung Baru enclave.

Publisher (U.S.): Michelle Bisson
Writers: Heidi Munan, Foo Yuk Yee, and Jo-Ann Kee-Spilling
Editors: Deborah Grahame-Smith, Stephanie Pee
Copyreader: Tara Tomczyk
Designers: Nancy Sabato, Benson Tan
Cover picture researcher: Tracey Engel
Picture researcher: Joshua Ang

Marshall Cavendish Benchmark
99 White Plains Road
Tarrytown, NY 10591
Website: www.marshallcavendish.us

© Times Media Private Limited 1990. First Edition.
© Times Media Private Limited 2002. Second Edition.
© Marshall Cavendish International (Asia) Private Limited 2012. Third Edition.
® "Cultures of the World" is a registered trademark of Times Publishing Limited.

Originated and designed by Times Media Private Limited
An imprint of Marshall Cavendish International (Asia) Private Limited
A member of Times Publishing Limited

Marshall Cavendish is a trademark of Times Publishing Limited.

Library of Congress Cataloging-in-Publication Data
Munan, Heidi.
  Malaysia / Heidi Munan, Foo Yuk Yee, and Jo-Ann Spilling. — 3rd ed.
    p. cm. — (Cultures of the world)
  Includes bibliographical references and index.
  Summary: Provides comprehensive information on the geography, history, wildlife, governmental structure, economy, cultural diversity, peoples, religion, and culture of Malaysia"—Provided by publisher.
  ISBN 978-1-60870-785-0 (print)
  1. Malaysia—Juvenile literature. I. Foo, Yuk Yee. II. Spilling, Jo-Ann. III. Title. IV. Series.

DS592.M85 2012
959.5—dc22   2011004468

Printed in Malaysia
7 6 5 4 3 2 1

CONTENTS

MALAYSIA TODAY

SITUATED IN SOUTHEASTERN ASIA, MALAYSIA LIES JUST NORTH
of the equator. It is one of the most developed and economically successful
nations in the region today. The country consists of two parts: East Malaysia
(Sabah and Sarawak) and West Malaysia (Peninsular Malaysia or Malaysian Borneo).
Thailand lies to the north of Peninsular Malaysia, whereas the island state of
Singapore lies at its southern tip. The South China Sea separates Peninsular Malaysia
from East Malaysia, which is located on the Indonesian island of Borneo.
Malaysia consists of 13 states and 3 federal territories.

Malaysia practices parliamentary democracy with a constitutional monarch who
bears the title Yang di-Pertuan Agong (head of state and customarily referred to as
the king) and who is elected from among nine hereditary state rulers (Conference
of Rulers) for a five-year term as the ceremonial head of state. In 2007 Malaysia
celebrated 50 years of independence from the British.

Malaysia is endowed with natural resources. It has large reserves of petroleum
and natural gas and is a leading exporter of tin, rubber, palm oil, and tropical
hardwoods. Known as one of Asia's tiger economies, Malaysia has grown rapidly—at

an annual rate of about 10 percent—since the 1970s. However, its economy, like many across the world today, has experienced a downturn because of the global financial crisis, which began in 2008. Malaysia is an important member of the Pacific Rim organization APEC (Asia-Pacific Economic Forum) and ASEAN (the Association of Southeast Asian Nations).

The world's tallest twin towers—the Petronas Towers located in the capital city of Kuala Lumpur—is a strong symbol of Malaysia's many economic achievements as well as its continued aspiration to be a fully developed country by the year 2020.

Malaysia's history has been shaped by the Portuguese and the Dutch in the 18th century, the British in the late 18th century until 1942, and the Japanese during World War II. Malaysia's past has contributed to its ethnic and cultural diversity today.

Malaysia's multicultural population makes it a vibrant and colorful country. The Malays, Chinese, and Indians, together with their different languages, religions, festivals, and cuisines, offer visitors a unique experience.

The iconic Petronas Towers.

Dancers in colorful costumes, performing during Kuala Lumpur City Day.

The government encourages intermingling among the three major ethnic groups to promote understanding, and all races live peacefully together.

Malaysians effortlessly combine the old ways with the new—they preserve their culture and religion by going to temples and mosques, but happily embrace modern technology in their workplace. Malaysians practice Eastern customs but are just as comfortable socializing and conducting business with people from Western countries. Because the British ruled this Crown colony until 1942, English is widely spoken and understood by many Malaysians. However, the way English is spoken can be very different from British English.

Malaysia offers those who live there a relaxed lifestyle. Malaysians mostly enjoy sunny tropical weather, although it can sometimes be too hot and humid for both visitors and locals alike. Malaysians who live in the larger towns and cities reside in houses and high-rise apartments or condominiums. In the capital city of Kuala Lumpur, the living standard is generally quite high, more or less like in any other major city in the world.

Malaysians, especially those who live in urban areas, have access to good health care, schools, highways, and communication systems. The use of the

A family picnicking in Templer Park.

Internet and mobile telephones is common in Malaysia. In Kuala Lumpur and other larger towns, people enjoy a range of cultural and leisure activities, including shopping, theater, cinema, and various indoor and outdoor sports. In the more rural areas Malaysians enjoy a slower and simpler pace of life. Those who live in the countryside spend their leisure time enjoying the many beautiful beaches, fishing, swimming, and other outdoor pursuits.

Malaysia's natural and diverse beauty makes it an attractive place to visit. There is much to explore and experience in Malaysia—from modern cities with impressive skyscrapers to elegant mosques, ancient temples, lush tropical rain forests, dense jungle, magnificent mountains, prehistoric caves, unusual wildlife, and exotic flora and fauna. Malaysia's favorite beach resorts include Pulau Langkawi, Pulau Tioman, and the Perhentian Islands. The national parks both in the Peninsula as well as in east Malaysia draw many visitors, too.

Malaysia is a haven for food-lovers. The local cuisine is delicious, but visitors who prefer other kinds of food can choose from a wide range of international cuisines, from American fast food to European specialties. Malaysians have a great appreciation of food and organize their social lives

A food stall in an outdoor night market.

around food—either eating out in a popular restaurant or enjoying a simple meal at home.

Although there have been racial tensions among the main ethnic groups at different times throughout the country's history, most Malaysians live in harmony and respect one another's religious beliefs and customs. In general the people of Malaysia have managed to put aside their ethnic differences to forge a distinctive Malaysian identity. Today many are beginning to feel a sense of national identity and are proud to be Malaysians.

The main idea behind "Vision 2020" is that Malaysia should be a fully developed country by 2020, but that success should not be measured merely by economic progress. According to Malaysia's longest-serving Prime Minister Tun Dr. Mahathir bin Mohamad, the country must aim to be "a nation that is fully developed along all the dimensions: economically, politically, socially, spiritually, psychologically and culturally."

The future success of Malaysia ultimately lies in its people's ability to embrace this vision and develop a nation where there is social cohesion, social justice, political stability, a system of government, and a good quality of life for every Malaysian.

GEOGRAPHY

An aerial view of Sempurna Bay in Sabah.

1

THE TWO PARTS OF MALAYSIA—East Malaysia (consisting of the states of Sabah and Sarawak) and West Malaysia (also known as Peninsular Malaysia)—make up a total land area of 127,355 square miles (330,242 square kilometers), slightly larger than the state of New Mexico.

Malaysia is the 66th-largest country in the world in terms of land area. East Malaysia makes up around 60 percent of the total land area of the country, whereas West Malaysia makes up the remaining 40 percent. East and West Malaysia are separated by about 400 miles (640 km) of the South China Sea.

In the days of sailing ships in the 15th and 16th centuries, harbors along the Straits of Melaka and on the southern tip of the Malay Peninsula were used by traders during the monsoon season as safe ports in which to weather the storms in the South China Sea.

SEASONS

Although Malaysia is hot and humid for most of the year, it does in fact have

Right: An aerial view of the city of Kuala Lumpur.

Boys running through a tropical downpour.

two seasons—the dry season and rainy season. Rain falls daily during the monsoon season, which has its peak during the months from November to February, but even during the drier part of the year (May to September), there are a couple of rain showers a week. Peninsular Malaysia receives an average rainfall of around 118 inches (300 centimeters), whereas East Malaysia receives 200 inches (508 cm) a year. Kuala Lumpur records an average of 195 rainy days a year and Kota Kinabalu 183. But Kuching holds the record with 247 rainy days a year! The daily average humidity is around 90 percent in Malaysia. Temperatures range from 77°F (25°C) to 95°F (32°C), with mostly cool nights. "Cool" means that in hilly areas it is advisable to sleep under a light blanket. A cotton sheet is enough for sleepers in the low-lying areas.

PENINSULAR MALAYSIA

The 13 states of Peninsular Malaysia extend from the state of Johor at the southern tip of the peninsula (separated from Singapore by the Straits of Johor) to the Thai border in the north. These states include several offshore islands, including Langkawi, Redang, Tioman, and Pangkor.

Banjaran Titiwangsa is a mountain range that forms the backbone of the Malay Peninsula. It runs from north to south, with short rivers draining into either the Straits of Melaka to the west or the South China Sea to the east. Its length is 298 miles (480 km) from north to south. Mount Kinabalu—the highest peak in Peninsular Malaysia—is a serious obstacle to east-west traffic. A road from Kuala Lumpur in the west to Kuantan in the east was completed in 1911 and another to Kota Bharu in 1982. In 1994 the North—South Expressway (NSE), the longest expressway in Malaysia, was completed.

Constructed in phases over a period of seven years, the NSE was officially opened on September 8, 1994, connecting western Peninsular Malaysia from Johor in the south to the northernmost state of Kedah. The expressway links many major cities and towns in western Peninsular Malaysia by providing a faster alternative to the old federal route, thus reducing traveling time between various towns and cities.

All the 13 states have access to the sea, from the 307 square miles (810 square km) of tiny Perlis Indera Kayangan, tucked away between Kedah Darul Aman and Thailand, to the 13,886 square miles (35,965 square km) of majestic Pahang Darulmakmur in the center of the peninsula. Kedah is a land of fertile plains devoted to rice growing, whereas huge estates of oil palm, cocoa, and rubber are found in the lowlands of Johor.

The states of Kelantan and Terengganu are east of the main mountain range. Undulating plains lie open to the South China Sea, which traditionally provides a living for the fearless fishermen who live in these states. Perak, Selangor, and Negeri Sembilan occupy the western coast south of Kedah. Tin ore is found in these three states, which gave them corresponding political and economic importance in the 19th century. Melaka (or Malacca) was a major trading port until the arrival of the Portuguese in 1511. Pulau Pinang (Penang Island) rose to prominence as a port in the late 18th century.

The island of Langkawi is a popular tourist destination.

SABAH AND SARAWAK

East Malaysia lies on the island of Borneo, north of the Indonesian province of Kalimantan. The two East Malaysian states, Sarawak and Sabah, are separated from Peninsular Malaysia by the South China Sea about 373 miles (600 km) away. Until recent times rivers were the most common transportation routes in both states, and the main settlements were within the tidal estuaries. Early exports included jungle produce and birds' nests.

The island of Borneo.

Sabah occupies 28,765 square miles (73,711 square km) of Borneo's northeastern corner. Its profile is dominated by the Crocker Range (where Mount Kinabalu stands), which extends toward the south, forming the watershed between Sarawak and Kalimantan. Sabah's main rivers drain into the Sulu Sea, where Sandakan (Sabah's first capital) is situated. Sabah's capital, Kota Kinabalu, is located on Sabah's western coast against the backdrop of the majestic Mount Kinabalu.

Of Sarawak's total land area of 48,050 square miles (124,450 square km), only about one-fifth is suitable for agriculture. Wide tracts of mangrove swamps or semi-saline swamp forest on the coast are sources of many natural products but are otherwise agriculturally unproductive. Kuching, the largest city and the capital of Malaysia's largest state, Sarawak, is located in Sarawak's western corner at the banks of the Sarawak River.

KUALA LUMPUR

Kuala Lumpur, the capital of Malaysia, began as a Chinese tin-mining settlement belonging to the Sultan of Selangor. The original township stood where the Gombak and Kelang rivers merged to form a delta. Hence the name Kuala Lumpur: *kuala* means "delta," a feature that forms where rivers meet or flow into the sea; *lumpur* means "muddy."

Present-day Kuala Lumpur is a modern city equipped with a generally efficient infrastructure, large shopping complexes, and first-class hotels. Its population is approximately 1,809,699 (according to a 2009 estimate). Taxis, mini- and omnibuses, and the monorail serve the transportation needs of locals and tourists alike. However, drainage is still a problem in low-lying areas. Traffic comes to a standstill when heavy monsoon rains cause flash floods. In 2008 the Kuala Lumpur City Hall (KLCH) and the Department of Drainage and Irrigation established a Master Plan to improve drainage and mitigate flooding in the capital and surrounding areas. Some of the proposed measures include the introduction of detention ponds, expanding drain sizes, and enhancing culverts.

Kuala Lumpur is a federal territory administered separately from its parent state, Selangor. Centrally located on the western coast of the Malay Peninsula, Kuala Lumpur is the center of the Malaysian federal government. The national university, the national palace, the national mosque, and the head offices of most big businesses are also located here. Kuala Lumpur is famous for being the home to the tallest twin buildings in the world—the Petronas Twin Towers (1,483 feet or 452 meters high).

The Al-Asyikin Mosque, with the Petronas Towers in the background, in Kuala Lumpur.

PENANG

Pulau Pinang (Penang Island), founded by Captain Francis Light of the British East India Company in the 18th century, was an important trading station in the Malay Peninsula until the 19th century. It declined in importance when Singapore, off the southern tip of the peninsula, rose to prominence in the 1820s.

Penang had a good natural harbor where ship captains could wait out the fierce monsoons, do a little quiet trading in Kedah, Perlis, Perak, or Sumatra, and then return to Calcutta in India after the winds had changed.

The population of Penang stands at approximately 1,773,442 (according to a 2010 estimate). Penang's industries include rubber processing, textile manufacture, and food production. Tin from Perak and southern Thailand is smelted in Penang, and Thai rice is imported in bulk and redistributed throughout Malaysia from Penang. However, Penang's economy still relies heavily on commerce and tourism. Tourists flock to Penang to enjoy its rich cultural heritage and its beautiful tropical beaches.

Ferries regularly ply between George Town on the island of Penang and the town of Butterworth on the mainland. Regular air service also links Penang to the peninsula and the rest of the world.

The world's sixth-longest bridge (an 8.4-mile- or 13.5-km-long, three-lane, dual carriageway) now connects Penang to Province Wellesley on the mainland. The Malaysian prime minister opened the bridge in 1985 by driving across it in a Malaysia-made car, the Proton Saga.

A city monorail passes over traffic.

TRANSPORTATION

The peninsula has one of the best road systems in the region. Its major highways include the North-South Expressway and the East-West Link Expressway. Both these expressways connect all the main towns and cities in the peninsula, including Johor Bahru in the south, Port Kelang in the west, Kuantan in the east, and Koto Bharu in the north. Malaysia is also part of the Great Asian Highway project, which is working toward improving the road systems throughout the region.

Rail transportation is also well developed on the peninsula. There are two main lines and several brand lines throughout the peninsula. The West Coast line runs from the independent republic of Singapore, which lies to the south of the peninsula to Perlis in the north. The East Coast line runs from Gemas in the western state of Negeri Sembilan to Tumpat in the eastern state of Kelantan. In East Malaysia there is a rail line only between Kota Kinabalu and Tenom in Sabah. Coastal and sea transportation systems in Malaysia are important, given the country's long coastline. Coastal and river ports include George Town and Port Kelang in Peninsular Malaysia and Kuching, Sibu, Labuan, Kota Kinabalu, Sandakan, and Tawau in East Malaysia.

Air transportation is growing rapidly and is an important link between East and Peninsular Malaysia, with regular internal services between Kuala Lumpur, Kuching, and Kota Kinabalu. A fleet of small aircrafts also maintains vital links in the remote areas of East Malaysia. There are international airports in Johor Bahru, Kuala Lumpur, and Penang. Built on 24,711 acres (10,000 hectares), the modern Kuala Lumpur International Airport was completed in 1998. High-speed trains connect the airport to the city center.

River transportation, the traditional mode of transportation in Malaysia, remains important for some settlements in Sabah and Sarawak. This is because East Malaysia does not have as extensive a network of roads as Peninsular Malaysia, where river transportation has lost its importance except in parts of the eastern coast.

Flooded trees and mangroves in the Bako National Park.

NATIONAL PARKS AND WILDLIFE

Taman Negara, Malaysia's best-known national park, is situated in the state of Pahang in the center of the Peninsular Malaysia. Set in 1,677 square miles (4,343 square km) of dense tropical forest surrounding the East Coast Range, the Taman Negara encompasses Gunung Kinabalu and spans across three states: Kelantan, Terengganu, and Pahang.

The Taman Negara can be reached only by river. There are no roads leading directly into the park. Kuala Tembeling is the last stop for travelers by road and rail. From there visitors have to travel by boat to Kuala Tahan and the chalet-style lodgings at the foot of the mountain.

Flora and fauna are painstakingly preserved in the Taman Negara, making the park a paradise for bird-watchers, butterfly hunters (armed with a camera), simian fanciers, or adventure seekers who enjoy the thrill of getting

Mount Kinabalu attracts many nature and hiking enthusiasts every year.

close to a tiger or a wild buffalo—both rare but still found in this national park. The park is home to around 1,400 species of plants, 250 species of birds, and around 200 mammals.

Sarawak's oldest national park, the Bako National Park—spanning an area of 6,739 acres (2,727 ha)—preserves a slice of coastal and lowland forests for future generations. Moreover the Niah National Park protects spectacular limestone outcroppings within which the giant Niah caves are concealed. No national park in Malaysia is easy to reach, and the 7,668-acre (3,140-ha) Niah is no exception. A bumpy 112-mile (180-km) drive from Miri takes visitors to Batu Niah. From there it is a short boat ride to Pengkalan Lobang. Finally a 2.5-mile (4-km) walk through the park, partly on a plank, brings visitors to the caves' western entrance. In 1958 archaeologists discovered evidence of human occupation of the caves dating back some 40,000 years at Niah.

MOUNT KINABALU

At 13,435 feet (4,101 m), Mount Kinabalu is the highest peak in Southeast Asia. Rising within view of the sea, it actually seems to be "near as high as Mount Everest," as a startled World War II pilot described it when the huge mass suddenly appeared in front of his fragile craft.

Mount Kinabalu is the center of one of Malaysia's most popular national parks, the Kinabalu National Park in Sabah. The park's 306 square miles (4,343 square km) include lowland rain forest, hill forest, "cloud forest" (mossy vegetation shrouded in mist and moisture), subalpine grass patches, and bare, wind-scrubbed granite near the summit.

The Kinabalu National Park is a botanist's dream. The parasitic plant Rafflesia, with its 3-feet (1-m) bloom, is found here, as are many varieties of fungi, including the "sunburst," and fern trees 13 feet (4 m) high. Ground orchids, tree orchids, cliff orchids, and the tiny Podochilus, which is just barely visible to the naked eye, all grow wild in this park. The rain forest of the Kinabalu National Park teems with nepenthes, graceful pitcher plants that hold up to 7 pints (3 liters) of liquid and trap live insects in their depths.

Malaysia's wildlife is well represented in this park. Bats and squirrels, shrews and tarsiers, and the slow loris make their home here. Monkeys and apes, including the friendly orangutan, thrive in this protected area. The pangolin, a scaly anteater, is safe here from greedy gourmets, as are the deer, boars, and more than 300 species of birds.

INTERNET LINKS

www.geographia.com/malaysia/nationalparks.htm

This website provides useful and detailed information about the main national parks in Malaysia, including Taman Negara, Beko, Endau-Rompin, Niah, Kinabalu, Gunung Mulu, Kuala Gula Bird Sanctuary, Tunku Abdul Rahman, Rantau Abang Turtle Sanctuary, and more.

www.tourism.gov.my

This website provides an overview of activities visitors can do, including exploring Malaysia's stunning national parks, ecotourism, agro-tourism, bird-watching, and cave exploration.

www.malaysia-wildlife-and-nature.com

This website provides information on the varied wildlife that can be found in Malaysia, including the Malayan tiger, sea turtles, exotic birds, butterflies, dragonflies, and more. Furthermore this website gives details of birding sites and turtle sanctuaries in addition to offering information about Malaysia's mountains and lakes.

HISTORY

Port de Santiago was a fort built by the Portuguese in Melaka.

2

EARLY PEOPLE LEFT CLUES THAT tell us a lot about the way they lived and the things they did. Pieces of broken pottery (also known as potsherds), worked stone and wood fragments, traces of villages and towns, and cave paintings are just some of the physical manifestations of early habitation.

In Malaysia such precious materials are vulnerable to destruction in the warm and humid climate. The moisture-laden atmosphere speeds up the rate at which raw wood rots and metals rust, and creeping plants

A dolmen, a prehistoric monument where two or more stones are erected, in the Kelabit Highlands in Borneo, Sarawak. A chieftain is thought to have been buried here.

A carving of a powerful headhunter in the Kelabit Highlands.

and mosses soon shroud stone structures. Thus Malaysia's prehistory has been pieced together from accidental discoveries of ancient objects in caves, burial sites, and ritual deposits in dry, gravelly soils. Nevertheless what is known is fascinating.

In 1958 an archaeological exploration led by Brian Harrison and his team unearthed a human skull that was estimated to be 40,000 years old. Red-earth paintings on the cave walls show men paddling boats and hunting animals, and a scene resembling a dance. Boat-shaped coffins from a later date have also been found, which were thought to ship the dead down "the big river" into the next world.

Little is known about the early Niah people, but it is certain that they had developed crafts such as pottery and simple weaving. Pottery and stone implements have been found in Gua Cha, a cave in Kelantan. Fragments of rough boats hauled up into dry shelters show that the early settlers built usable craft using stone tools.

EARLY ASIAN CONTACTS

Strategically located midway between India and China, the Malay Peninsula provides a natural trading interchange between these two giants. It is believed that traders met and exchanged goods in sheltered places along the Straits of Melaka and around the peninsula's southern tip centuries before any ship was prepared to undertake the entire long and dangerous voyage between Calcutta and ports in China such as Hangzhou.

Over the centuries foreign traders and settlers brought their religions and ways of life with them, although they did not settle in significant numbers. Hinduism and Buddhism left cultural traces in artifacts and in customs that were absorbed into local folkways. For instance many Malay wedding customs have their origin in a dim Hindu past. Cheng Hoon Teng, Malaysia's oldest traditional Chinese temple, is dedicated to Admiral Cheng Ho or Zheng He, who visited Melaka in 1405. As more Chinese settled in Malaysia, a unique mix of Chinese and Malay cultures occurred, and the Straits Chinese, or Peranakans, were born.

MELAKA

The foundation of the first powerful state in the Straits of Melaka is shrouded in legend. A young prince or princeling named Parameswara, exiled from his native Sumatra (now part of Indonesia), set up a pirate base on Temasek (the former name of the island of Singapore). Being a less than popular ruler, he was later expelled and fled to the fishing village of Melaka, where he made himself master around 1400.

A fortuitous geographic position and the trade patterns of the day assisted Parameswara's undoubted abilities. Melaka grew into a trading center that was important enough to attract the jealousy of the Siamese, as well as the protection of China, the distant overlord of most of Southeast

Chinese traders joined the early settlements to exchange Chinese goods for Indian ones and to buy the peninsula's produce. It is from Chinese historians that we know what goods were in demand, at what prices, and how the people of the Malay Peninsula dressed and behaved.

The early port in Melaka was a bustling one.

The founding of Singapore in 1819 and the Anglo-Dutch Treaty of 1824 gave Great Britain control of the Straits of Melaka. Laborers were imported from India and China to work in tin mines and rubber plantations. In the 1870s local conflicts gave the British an excuse to install "advisers" in the sultans' courts. These British officials ruled the states except for matters of religion and local custom. In 1896 Perak, Pahang, Selangor, and Negeri Sembilan were persuaded to unite as the Federated Malay States for administrative convenience.

The Indian and Chinese communities became more prominent in the 1920s. Anti-British Chinese political parties were founded. Malay nationalism stirred. Each community was suspicious of every other, but relied on the British to keep order.

Malaya, as the peninsula was then known, consisted of the Federated and Unfederated Malay States under British protection and the Straits Settlements of Penang, Melaka, and Singapore, which were British colonies.

The Japanese invaded Malaya in 1941, on the same day they bombed Pearl Harbor. They surrendered to the Allies, which included the British, in 1945.

Asia during that time. Numerous Indian traders settled in Melaka. They brought Islam to the Straits in the early 15th century. The history of Melaka under its Indianized Malay court offers many examples of intrigue and heroism.

Melaka's last chief minister, Tun Mutahir, made the fatal mistake of trying to trick the Portuguese when they sailed into the Straits in 1509. He launched a sneak attack on the foreign vessels in the port. Most of the intruders escaped, only to return with reinforcements to take revenge on the treacherous "Moors," as they called all Muslims.

WESTERN CONTACTS

Portugal was the first Western nation to raise its flag in the Straits of Melaka. The Portuguese took control of Melaka in 1511 and built a fort, a church, and a customs house.

Things were not rosy for the Portuguese. The exiled sultan of Melaka, having established himself in Johor on the southern tip of the peninsula, was trying to regain his dominion.

Other powerful Malay states in the region resented the Christian intruders' attempts to create a trade monopoly. Sea rovers and pirates were encouraged to attack foreign shipping vessels. Rather than risk taking the route through the pirate-infested Straits of Melaka, bigger and better-equipped vessels chose to sail west of Sumatra on their way to Batavia in the Dutch East Indies. As a result legitimate trade declined.

The Dutch, who had established themselves in western Java in the early 17th century, defeated the Portuguese in Melaka in 1641, and the town's importance declined rapidly after the British acquired Penang from the sultan of Kedah in 1786 and Melaka from the Dutch in 1824 through the Anglo-Dutch Treaty. Penang became the only important foreign trading base in the Straits.

THE INGREDIENTS OF MALAYSIA

The Malayan Emergency was declared in mid-1948 when the Malayan Communist Party (MCP) embarked on a systematic campaign of violence against European interests. The communists were mainly Chinese and received substantial support from their rural compatriots. After 1950 British forces gained control by resettling these communities into "New Villages," thus denying the MCP access to supplies. The emergency officially ended in 1960.

The main reason for the communist insurrection's failure was a new alliance between Malay and Chinese leaders and Great Britain's commitment to Malaya's independence. Malaya's first elections were held in 1955, in preparation for independence in 1957. Three parties emerged: the United Malays National Organization (UMNO), the Malaysian Chinese Association (MCA), and the Malaysian Indian Congress (MIC). The first elected prime minister was from the Kedah aristocracy, Tunku Abdul Rahman.

In the early 1960s a new, larger federation was proposed: Malaysia, including Malaya and Singapore, and Brunei, Sarawak, and Sabah on the island of Borneo. Brunei, Sarawak, and Sabah became British colonies after World War II. Before that Sarawak had been ruled by the family of James Brooke, known as the White Rajahs. Sabah had been ruled by a chartered company founded by the British—the British North Borneo Company—and foreign trade interests. James Brooke was an Englishman and a merchant mariner. In 1825 he used his large inheritance to purchase a 142-ton (129-metric-ton) schooner, *The Royalist*.

Former chief minister of Malaya, Tunku Abdul Rahman (1903–1990), seated, second from right signs the final document of the Federation of Malaya Constitutional Conference.

He sailed for the island of Borneo to make his fortune. When he arrived in 1838 he helped the sultan quell the unrest that was created by the Dayak people. As a reward for his service, the sultan appointed him governor of Sarawak on September 24, 1941. James Brooke eventually established an independent rule over the territory, and the sultan recognized him as Rajah of Sarawak on August 18, 1842.

In the end Brunei chose not to join the federation. The British government granted Sabah and Sarawak independence through joining the Federation of Malaysia, which was declared in 1963. Singapore left Malaysia in 1965 to become an independent republic.

Postwar Malaysia was marked by the political drive of the Malays, expressed through the UMNO party. However, Malay dominance also caused bitterness and racial antagonism, resulting in the deaths of hundreds of people during the 1969 racial riots in Kuala Lumpur. Although just over half of the population was ethnic Malay, only 1.5 percent of company assets in the country were owned by Malays, and per capita income among Malays was less than half that of non-Malays. In light of this a policy in favor of

Malays, called the New Economic Policy (NEP), was introduced in the 1970s to help even out this economic inequality. The Malays and the indigenous peoples of Malaysia were offered privileges in business, education, property development, and government, and were classified as *bumiputera* (boo-MI-put-teh-RAH), or "sons of the soil." The NEP has caused some resentment among the non-Malays, who are loath to invest wholeheartedly in a country where they face discrimination. Partly because of its unpopularity among non-Malays, the NEP was terminated in 1990. The NEP was replaced by the National Development Policy, which shares some of the aims of the NEP.

INTERNET LINKS

www.historyofnations.net/asia/malaysia.html

This website provides a brief summary of the history of Malaysia from the first century A.D. to the present. In addition the site provides useful details on significant periods of Malaysia's history, including its prehistoric times to its days under the powerful Portuguese, Dutch, and British empires.

www.melaka.net/history1.htm

This website provides a comprehensive account of the story of Melaka, including information about the key figures who have shaped Melaka's history, such as Parameswara, Chinese Admiral Cheng Ho or Zheng He, Munshi Abdullah, and others. This site also offers views on Melaka's importance as a thriving intermediary and the part it played in the spice trade.

www.colonialvoyage.com/malacca.html

This site provides the history of Melaka under the colonial rule of the Portuguese and the Dutch. Browsers can view interesting accounts of Portuguese rule from 1511 to 1641, followed by Dutch rule from 1641 to 1795 and 1818 to 1825, in addition to useful photographs and maps.

The formation of Malaysia in 1963 led to serious regional tensions, especially with Indonesia. In September that year Indonesia launched a campaign of "confrontation," with commandos infiltrating Sabah and Sarawak. This achieved nothing, and hostilities ceased in 1966.

GOVERNMENT

The Malaysian Parliament building in Kuala Lumpur.

MALAYSIA HAS A PARLIAMENTARY democracy with a constitutional monarch who is a nonpolitical Supreme Head of the country known as the Yang di-Pertuan Agong (young di-per-twan ah-gohng). Each member state has its own legislature. For example Sabah and Sarawak have their own immigration laws, so a passport is needed when traveling between East and Peninsular Malaysia.

CONSTITUTION

The federal constitution of Malaysia represents the supreme law of the nation. The constitution guarantees every Malaysian citizen basic democratic and human rights such as the right to life, freedom of movement, freedom of speech, and freedom of religion. Under Malaysian law the constitution may be amended by a two-thirds majority in the parliament. The drafting of the constitution in January 1956 marked an important milestone in Malaysia's history, as it was the first step toward the formation of a new government after Great Britain agreed to concede independence to Malaya.

In the first federal election in 1955, Tunku Abdul Rahman was appointed chief minister, heading a delegation to London in 1956 to discuss the federal constitution and negotiate the date for the

3

Malaysia is made up of a federation of 13 states and 3 federal territories. It is a parliamentary democracy and operates on a multiparty system.

independence of Malaya. It was finally agreed that the constitution would commence on August 31, 1957.

PARLIAMENT

The federal parliament consists of two chambers, the House of Representatives and the Senate. The House of Representatives consists of 222 members who serve for a period of 5 years. The Senate consists of 70 members. Representatives are elected by the people; senators are mainly appointed by the Yang di-Pertuan Agong or elected by the state legislatures. The parliament is the legislative arm of the government. It formulates all the laws of Malaysia in addition to acting as an approving body for government expenditure and taxes. The party that commands a majority in the parliament chooses the prime minister, or *perdana menteri* (per-DAH-nah men-teh-ri), although he is officially appointed by the Yang di-Pertuan Agong. The perdana menteri chooses his party members in the House of Representatives or Senate to be ministers in charge of various ministerial portfolios, such as health or transport. This cabinet is responsible to the parliament and ultimately to the electorate. In the United States one person—the president—fulfills both executive and ceremonial functions. In Malaysia, however, the two functions are separate: The perdana menteri is the chief executive of the nation and the Yang di-Pertuan Agong is the ceremonial head of state.

GOVERNANCE

Under the constitution power is shared among the executive, judicial, and legislative authorities. The head of the executive authority is the monarch, the Yang di-Pertuan Agong. The prime minster and his cabinet of ministers serve

The National Monument, designed by the creator of the Iwo Jima Memorial in Washington, D.C., was constructed in 1966 to commemorate the nation's heroes.

on the executive authority. The legislative authority holds the power to make the laws of the nation. It is made up of the Yang di-Pertuan Agong, members of the House of Representatives, and the Senate. The head of the judicial authority is the chief justice of the Federal Court of Malaysia. The Federal Court has the power to question or overturn any law made by the parliament. Judicial authority is carried out through superior courts (including federal, appeal, and high courts of Malaya and Borneo) and lower subordinate courts (including magistrate, shariah, and juvenile courts).

STATE GOVERNMENTS AND FEDERAL TERRITORIES

There are 13 states in Malaysia—Johor, Kedah, Kelantan, Melaka, Negeri Sembilan, Pahang, Perak, Perlis, Penang, Sabah, Sarawak, Selangor, and Terengganu—as well as 3 federal territories—Kuala Lumpur, Putrajaya, and Labuan.

Prime Minister Datuk Najib Tun Razak (*left*) and U.S. president Barack Obama (*right*) at the Nuclear Security Summit in Washington, D.C., in 2010.

The prime minister of Malaysia is appointed by the monarch and head of state, the Yang di-Pertuan Agong. The prime minister is head of the cabinet and a member of the House of Representatives. He appoints the cabinet ministers with approval from the Yang di-Pertuan Agong. The prime minster and his cabinet of ministers are jointly responsible to the parliament. The prime minister is expected to be supported by the majority of Malaysia's citizens.

Since independence in 1957 Malaysia has had six prime ministers. The first was Tunku Abdul Rahman (1957—69), affectionately known as the Father of Independence because he was instrumental in securing independence from the British. The second was Abdul Razak (1970—76), who gave Malaysia the New Economic Policy (NEP). The third was Tun Hussein Onn (1976—81), who was known as the Father of Unity. Malaysia's fourth and longest-serving prime minister was Tun Dr. Mahathir Mohamad (1981—2003, below). He served for 22 years and is responsible for the rapid economic growth and modernization of Malaysia. The fifth prime minister was Tun Abdullah Ahmad Badawi (2003—09). The current prime minister is Datuk Seri Najib Tun Razak, who took office in 2009.

Prime Minister Datuk Seri Najib Tun Razak inspects the delegates of ruling political party, UMNO, in 2010.

Each individual state has its own head of state and corresponding state government, consisting of municipal councils and statutory bodies. However, in the absence of a head of state, the federal territories are administered under the authorities of the Ministry of Federal Territories and Urban Wellbeing.

Both state assemblies and federal territories share the powers of government among the executive, judicial, and legislative authorities. These federal territories share equal status with other states in Malaysia, but they do not have a head of state or a state assembly.

The larger towns within each state have town boards, municipal councils, or city councils. These bodies administer planning, sanitation, and building bylaws; issue various licenses and permits; and collect fees for services, including garbage collection and road maintenance.

City and municipal councils may be appointed or elected; the process differs from state to state. The smallest administrative unit is the village or—in Sabah and Sarawak—the longhouse. A *ketua kampung* (keh-twah kahm-pohng), meaning "village elder," or *tuai rumah* (too-why roo-mah), meaning "house elder," presides over the village or longhouse community.

In some Chinese-populated areas, a *kapitan Cina* (kah-pi-tahn chee-nah), or Chinese elder, is appointed with similar limited functions.

An elder is usually appointed, although elders in the past were elected by the population under their jurisdiction. The rationale for these positions is that a person who is versed in traditional law and customs should deal with the small, ordinary matters that arise in the daily life of the community. In some ways the elders' functions resemble those of a justice of the peace.

The Sultan Abdul Samad building now houses the supreme and high courts.

The elder is in charge of the smooth functioning of his community. The elder directs sanitation projects and other community activities. In most states he can even impose small fines. However, he has limited judicial powers to settle family disputes and infringements of traditional law. Most everyday legal matters, such as the issuing of birth, marriage, and death certificates, are handled by the district offices.

LAW

Malaysians may not hold dual citizenship. Those who do so are liable to lose their Malaysian citizenship by process of law.

A Malaysian father remains the legal guardian of his children even if he has divorced their mother. Non-Muslim Malaysians under 21 years of age cannot get married if their parents object. If these objections are unreasonable, the couple may seek a court order to override their parents' objections or wait until both young people turn 21. Muslim women may marry once they turn 16; Muslim men may marry after age 18. Muslim marriages must be registered at least a week before the wedding and solemnized at a mosque.

Under the Internal Security Act, Malaysians may be detained without being charged in court if they are suspected of being a threat to public order or the security of the country. The death penalty is mandatory for those who are convicted of drug trafficking, and the criminal is usually executed within a few months of conviction.

The courts decide civil and criminal cases or settle the legality of any law or act of government that is questioned. To enable it to perform its work impartially, the judiciary is designed to be independent of political or any other interference.

INTERNET LINKS

www.malaysia.gov.my

This website provides current government initiatives and other relevant topics apart from helping citizens access services and public information. Browsers can also access relevant questionnaires, feedback forms, and public complaint forms.

www.pmo.gov.my

This website of the prime minister's office provides personal information concerning the prime minister and his actions, including his mission for the country. Additionally this website offers details on the work and activities of the prime minister's department, including press releases, speeches, customer charters, diary, news, initiatives, and links to useful resources.

www.lexadin.nl/wlg/legis/nofr/oeur/lxwemal.htm

This comprehensive website covers many aspects of legislation in Malaysia, including constitutional law, human rights, litigation and court procedure, electoral law, administrative law, public law, criminal law, civil law, commercial law, company law, labor law, health law, tax law, and more.

ECONOMY

A man tapping a rubber tree for its sap.
Rubber was one of Malaysia's top exports.

N 2007 MALAYSIA HAD THE 3rd-largest economy in South East Asia and the 30th-largest economy in the world by purchasing power parity. Purchasing power parity is an exchange rate that would make the cost of goods and services the same in two (or more) countries that are being compared.

MALAYSIA'S ECONOMY TODAY

In the 1970s Malaysia's economy was largely reliant on the production and export of raw materials. In 2009 its estimated gross domestic product (GDP) was $383.6 billion. Today, however, it has achieved its status as a healthy, newly industrialized country with a diversified economy. More than three-quarters of the country's population is urban after almost half a century of rapid rural-to-urban migration. The UN Statistics Division put Malaysia's rural-urban population distribution at a ratio of 28:72 in 2010, although the figures for rural dwellers are higher in Sabah and Sarawak. The national workforce totals 11.38 million people (according to a 2009 estimate). Malaysia's long-term goal is to become a fully developed nation by 2020. The 2020 vision aims to achieve balanced growth and a high quality of life. To ensure that the 2020 goal is on track the government launched the 10th Malaysia Plan (2011—15) in 2010. The main objectives include charting development for a high-income nation with healthy growth

4

Malaysia's economy is dependent on the export of electronics, oil, and gas as well as investments in high-technology industries, medical technology, and pharmaceuticals. It hopes to achieve the status of a fully developed country by 2020.

and full employment by creating a private sector-led economy and supporting innovation-led growth.

AGRICULTURE

Only 13 percent of the workforce is employed in agriculture, and the sector has been declining for years. For those who remain working in agriculture, it has been increasingly hard to earn a living because there have been challenging problems such as regular flooding and thin unproductive soil. However, a huge success story within the agriculture sector has been the production of palm oil. Malaysia is the second-largest palm oil producer in the world, employing more than half a million people. In 2008 Malaysia produced 17.7 million tons (15.5 metric tons) of crude palm oil. It is remarkable to mention that Malaysia is the world's second-largest exporter of palm oil, exporting it to countries that include the United States and China. Palm oil is used widely in cooking.

A woman sifting rice. The agricultural sector has been declining in Malaysia.

The country's long coastline—spanning 1,905 miles (4,675 km)—and numerous rivers and lakes present some opportunities for fishing, a common occupation in the more rural areas. Malaysia's fishing industry employs more than 100,000 people either directly or in processing plants.

Other agricultural products include rubber, cocoa, and rice. In East Malaysia subsistence crops, coconuts, pepper, and timber are produced. Homegrown timber and other tropical wood are made into furniture, veneer, and plywood for both local and international consumption.

MAIN INDUSTRIES

The biggest employers in Malaysia are the civil service, the service industry, and the manufacturing sector. A total of 57 percent of the labor force is employed in the services industry, and 36 percent work in manufacturing.

The latter includes petroleum refining, car assembly, and the processing of domestic raw materials, such as timber, rubber, and oil.

The main industries in Peninsular Malaysia are rubber and oil palm processing and manufacturing, light manufacturing, pharmaceuticals, medical technology, electronics, tin mining and smelting, logging, and timber processing. In Sabah the main industries are logging and petroleum production, whereas in Sarawak, they are petroleum production, refining, agriculture processing, and logging.

PETROLEUM AND LIQUEFIED NATURAL GAS play a major role in Malaysia's economy. Malaysia is the world's second-largest exporter of liquefied natural gas, and it has the third-highest oil reserves in the region.

Crude oil and natural gas are found in offshore fields in the South China Sea. The main oil-producing states are Terengganu in Peninsular Malaysia and Sabah and Sarawak. Natural gas found in offshore fields in the South China Sea is liquefied in Malaysia, and some crude oil is refined locally. Petroleum products, such as chemicals and plastics, are manufactured in Malaysia before being exported.

A worker at an oil palm plantation loading oil palm branches into carts to be transported to the refinery.

Malaysia's vast oil reserves are managed by the state-owned company Petronas. All production and exploration projects operate through Petronas, a company that contributes almost 40 percent toward the national revenue. As of January 2009 Malaysia had a total of 68 oil-producing fields, and its oil reserves reached 4 billion barrels. In 2008 total oil production was 727,000 barrels per day, whereas consumption in the same year reached an estimated 547,000 barrels per day and net exports about 180,000 barrels per day.

RUBBER Malaysia is the world's third-largest natural rubber producer, with an average annual rubber output of approximately 900,000 tons (816,466 metric tons). In 2009 Malaysia produced 857,019 tons (777,475 metric tons) and exported 703,051 tons (637,797 metric tons) of rubber. Malaysia is famous for being the world's largest supplier of rubber gloves.

TIN Tin still brings in a portion of Malaysia's foreign exchange earnings. The country's oldest known name, *Aurea Chersonesus*, means "peninsula of gold." Malaysia was the second-largest producer of refined tin in 1997. Most Malaysian tin is found in the states of Perak and Selangor. In recent times the tin industry has suffered as most of the country's extensive resources have been significantly depleted. In the mid-1980s Malaysia was mining more than 35,000 tons (31,751 metric tons) of tin metal and concentrates, but in 2004 Malaysia produced only 3,358 tons (3,046 metric tons). Although tin mining was once a large employer, the number of people employed in the industry is falling rapidly as there are fewer than 40 working mines in the country today.

CONSTRUCTION The health of Malaysia's construction industry fluctuates with the economic realities of the day. Although it was heavily hit by the global financial crisis, which began in 2008, the construction industry grew by 8.5 percent in the first quarter of 2010 with the help of a stimulus package provided by the government.

IRON AND STEEL Malaysia supports a thriving iron and steel industry and proudly produces its own automobiles. The Proton Saga car was launched in September 1985 by the then prime minister of Malaysia, Mahathir Bin Mohamad. Since its launch over 25 years ago, the Malaysian-made Proton Saga has received awards and has sold successfully in Malaysia as well as internationally.

Malaysia's economy relies heavily on the export of gas and oil, as well as of electronics. In an attempt to steer the economy away from its dependence on exports, the government is making efforts to promote domestic demand. Additionally the current government has put plans in place to attract investments in high-technology industries, pharmaceuticals, and medical technology.

TOURISM

Tourism is Malaysia's third-largest foreign exchange earner. The industry contributes around 7 percent to the gross national product. In the World Tourism Organization (WTO) ranking of 2010, Malaysia had developed into one of the world's most popular vacation spots, becoming the ninth most visited country in the world.

Ecotourists on a boat tour on the Kinabatagan River.

THE 1997 ASIAN FINANCIAL CRISIS

Before the Asian financial crisis hit the region in July 1997, Malaysia's economy, like many others in the region, had been enjoying a healthy period of sustained growth. For many Malaysians it felt like they were on their way to becoming a rich and fully developed country. However, shortly after the Thai baht was devalued in July 1997, the Malaysian ringgit was severely affected. By end of 1997 the Malaysian ringgit had lost half of its value, falling from above 2.50 to under 4.10 to the U.S. dollar. To prevent the currency from falling further, the then prime minister, Mahathir Mohamad, imposed strict capital controls to keep the value of Malaysian currency by pegging the ringgit at 3.80 against the U.S. dollar. Pegging is a method of stabilizing a country's currency by fixing its exchange rate to that of another country.

In 1998 the country entered its first recession, with all its economic sectors experiencing a downturn. The recession lasted many years, and it was only in 2005 that the crisis measures were finally removed and the Malaysian ringgit was liberated from the fixed exchange system.

Many visitors come to enjoy Malaysia's relaxed rural lifestyle, its exotic mix of spicy food, its excellent swimming and diving spots, and its uncrowded, unspoiled beaches. Visitors from the cash-rich island Republic of Singapore make up by far the greatest number of tourists to Malaysia each year: Thousands of Singaporeans cross the causeway to Johor Bahru on weekends and public holidays.

In 1999 Malaysia launched a new worldwide marketing campaign called "Malaysia, Truly Asia" that attracted 7.9 million visitors to Malaysia. In 2009 the number of visitors had increased to 23.6 million.

COTTAGE INDUSTRIES AND RETAIL COMMERCE

Every industry, however small, needs a license in Malaysia. In practice, however, some cottage industries flourish without much supervision.

Many people, particularly those from the lower-income groups, eke out a meager living by hawking—that is, by selling things in the streets.

Hawkers may sell cigarettes, soft drinks, secondhand clothing, and other small or factory-rejected goods. Many Malaysian towns have established hawkers' centers, but many hawkers prefer to ply their trade on footpaths, by roadsides, at bus stations, in parking lots, or wherever people congregate. Some street sellers bring their wares in a *trishaw*, a three-wheeled bicycle; others have a temporary stall to shelter them and their goods from the rain. However, many makeshift hawkers carry their goods in baskets or spread their goods on mats on the ground, ready to vanish if anybody objects to their presence or wants to see their license.

Some hawkers have a business license and earn respectable amounts of money. Many of them, however, are fly-by-night operators and take to their heels when they see a policeman approaching. Many Malaysian housewives prepare cakes and snacks for sale and set up small stalls outside their houses. During Ramadan—the Islamic month of fasting—whole night markets spring up, ready to feed the Muslims who are breaking their daily fast.

INTERNET LINKS

www.economywatch.com/world_economy/malaysia

This useful guide provides economic statistics and related links to information about Malaysia's trade, export, imports, economic growth, industry sectors, economic forecast, and economic development.

www.eia.doe.gov/cabs/Malaysia/Oil

This website by the U.S. Energy Information Administration offers independent statistics and analysis on Malaysia's oil and gas industry.

www.doingbusiness.org/Data/ExploreEconomies/Malaysia

This website provides useful data on the ease of doing business in Malaysia, including topics such as starting a business, getting credit, registering properties, enforcing contracts, paying taxes, protecting investors, and more.

ENVIRONMENT

Malaysia is home to lush greenery and the highest peak in Southeast Asia, Mount Kinabalu.

WITH MORE THAN 60 PERCENT of its land covered with rain forest, Malaysia is rich in plant and animal life. The country's forests are home to some 286 species of mammals, 746 species of birds, 218 species of amphibians, 379 species of reptiles, and 368 species of fish.

Around 15,500 species of flowering plants grow in Malaysia. Malaysia also boasts the world's tallest tropical tree and largest flower. The Tualang tree, with a base diameter of over 10 feet (3 m), reaches heights of around 262 feet (80 m). The Rafflesia flower, 3 feet (1 m) wide, holds a Guinness Book world record.

THE ENVIRONMENTAL SITUATION TODAY

Today the Malaysian rain forest is under threat. Agriculture, urban development, and other human activities continue to eat into virgin forest, bulldozing valuable trees and destroying animal habitats. Haze from forest fires harms the air, and industrial waste released into rivers poisons marine life. As a result there are 156 threatened species in Malaysia today. Many animals, such as orangutans, the Sumatran rhinoceros, elephants, tigers, and turtles, are now in danger of extinction. It has been estimated that if the pace of destruction of the rain forest continues, half of all mammals and 25 percent of all bird species in Peninsular Malaysia will cease to exist by 2020.

Malaysia is party to the following international environmental agreements on biodiversity: Biological Diversity, Climate Change, Climate

5

Malaysia boasts a natural environment that is rich with exotic flora and fauna. However, some of its wildlife is endangered and its pressing environmental concerns include air and water pollution and deforestation.

A turtle hatchery on Turtle Island in Sabah.

Change—Kyoto Protocol, Desertification, Endangered Species, Hazardous Wastes, Law of the Sea, Marine Life Conservation, Ozone Layer Protection, Ship Pollution, Tropical Timber 83, Tropical Timber 94, and Wetlands.

The Malaysian government, together with world conservation authorities, is taking stern measures to protect the country's endangered wildlife and ensure the preservation of the natural environment for future generations.

ENDANGERED WILDLIFE

THE MALAYAN TIGER Tiger numbers have fallen worldwide due to deforestation and poaching. The bones and other body parts of the tiger are used to make traditional medicines in Asia. In the early 1900s there were around 100,000 tigers in the world. Today exact figures are not known, but it is estimated that as few as 3,200 tigers survive in the wild.

The Indo-Chinese subspecies in Malaysia is commonly called the Malayan tiger. It was once a common sight in Peninsular Malaysia, but urban development has eaten into its living space and reduced its population drastically. These rare creatures can now be seen only in a few states and in the Taman Negara National Park. No tigers have been reported in Penang and Melaka. The WWF-Malaysia's Tigers Alive! project is working to prevent the extinction of the Malayan tiger.

TURTLES Turtles have existed since the Triassic period, more than 200 million years ago. Most species, such as the giant Mesozoic sea turtle Archelon, which reached some 8 feet (2.4 m) in diameter, are now extinct. Only four sea turtle species survive today, and all are on the endangered list. The leatherback, hawksbill, green, and olive ridley sea turtles nest on Malaysian beaches. The largest of these, the leatherback, together with the hawksbill, are critically endangered and are unlikely to escape extinction.

Some causes of the decline in turtle numbers include the human consumption of turtle eggs (which are valued as an aphrodisiac), accidental capture in fishing nets, marine pollution, and the loss of nesting grounds due to human activity in coastal areas. Conservationists try to preserve turtle populations by reburying turtle eggs in hatcheries.

THE SUMATRAN RHINOCEROS The Sumatran rhinoceros is the smallest of its kind, weighing up to 2,205 pounds (1,000 kilograms). It is a popular target among poachers who are motivated by a large Asian market for its horns, which are valued as an aphrodisiac. Sumatran rhinoceroses are the most endangered of all the Asian rhinoceros species. There are probably fewer than 300 in the world, most of them in Indonesia. Between 12 and 15 of these rhinoceroses still remain in Sabah in the Endau-Rompin National Park. Until adequate protection can be provided in the wild, captive breeding is the only hope for the survival of this species.

THE MALAYAN ELEPHANT The Malayan elephant is a subspecies of the Asian elephant. Asian elephants are found mainly in reserves in India and Southeast Asia. They have smaller tusks than their African counterparts and are thus not as intensively poached for ivory. Their decline has been mainly due to the destruction of their natural habitat for logging and other development. Domesticated elephants are often used to clear their own native homes to make way for agriculture. To protect the remaining elephants of Malaysia, the Kuala Gandah Elephant Sanctuary in Pahang was established in 1989 under the Department of Wildlife and National Parks, Malaysia, and manned by the Elephant Capture and Translocation Unit (ECTU). Due to the impressive efforts of the ECTU, the elephant population has increased from 500 in 1972 to 1,200 at present.

CURRENT ISSUES

WATER Malaysia is rich in water resources because it receives a high level of annual rainfall. Population growth and urbanization, industrialization,

THE ORANGUTAN

The orangutan—whose name means "man of the forest" in Malay—is humans' closest relative and Asia's only great ape. It is extremely intelligent, but sadly, it is one of the most endangered of Malaysian wildlife species. Over the last 20 years there has been a 40 percent decline in orangutan numbers and today there are only about 12,300 orangutans alive in the world. Orangutans are found only in Borneo and Sumatra. The animal's survival is constantly threatened by forest fires, logging, and poaching. The Sepilok Orangutan Sanctuary in Sabah—24,711 acres (10,000 ha) of virgin rain forest—gives orangutans space to roam and mate, free from human interference.

and the expansion of irrigated agriculture are imposing rapidly increasing demands and pressure on water resources, besides contributing to the rising water pollution. The poor management of water resources in the country is a cause for concern, and both the government and the people are being encouraged to use water more efficiently to ensure that there is always enough water to meet everyone's needs in the future.

Urbanization and industrialization are adding to the demand for clean water and yet at the same time are polluting Malaysia's natural water sources. Cleaning up polluted waterways is an expensive but urgent task, as 90 percent of Malaysia's water supply comes from lakes, rivers, and streams flowing from the highland forests.

Malaysia's water pollution problem started in the 1970s with the birth of the palm-oil processing industry. Factories released industrial waste into rivers, polluting the water and killing marine life. The continued expansion of industry means that Malaysia's natural waterways will never be safe from industrial pollutants. Domestic sewage discharge, land clearing, and livestock farming also contribute to water pollution in Malaysia.

AIR POLLUTION Air pollution in Malaysia is mainly a consequence of industrial and vehicular emissions. According to Malaysia's Department of Environment (DOE), 14 million motor vehicles were registered in 2004 that emitted approximately twice the amount of carbon monoxide, nitrogen oxides, hydrocarbons, and sulfur dioxide as a decade ago. In addition there are approximately 5 million motorcycles contributing to the air pollution in Malaysia.

Motor vehicles, industry, land clearing, and open burning have caused serious air pollution problems. In 1997, and more recently in 2005, smoke billowing from 11 million acres (4.5 million ha) of burning forest in Sumatra, Kalimantan, and Borneo left several countries in Southeast Asia breathing noxious air for months. Airports, offices, factories, shops, and schools were closed, and Sarawak's residents were advised to stay home or wear protective masks. The pollution became so severe that from August 11 to August 13, 2005, a state of emergency was declared. Even Port Klang, one of the world's busiest ports, had to be closed due to poor visibility.

The number of cases of respiratory disease more than doubled in Kuala Lumpur during the haze of 1997 and 2005. Besides intensifying respiratory ailments, the haze may have long-term effects. Incomplete combustion of organic matter, such as trees and fossil fuels, releases polycyclic aromatic hydrocarbons (PAHs) into the atmosphere. The haze caused by raging forest fires in Indonesia exposed people to PAHs, some of which can cause cancer. When industrial and traffic emissions mix with PAHs, the overall effect can be lethal.

DEFORESTATION According to the UN, the pace of deforestation in Malaysia is accelerating faster than that of any other tropical country in the world. Figures show that between the periods 1990 and 2000 and 2000 and 2005, the deforestation rate was an alarming 86 percent. Since 2000 an average of 346,442 acres (140,200 ha) of forest area has been damaged.

As one of the top exporters of timber in the world, Malaysia continues to damage and deplete its rain forests to meet the increasing demand for tropical hardwoods among industrialized nations. As the most populous nations become wealthier, they will add even more to the global consumption of wood products. This rapid deforestation has contributed to land degradation—the wearing down of the soil and depletion of its nutrients. Deforestation and logging removes vegetation cover and makes

Urban development continues to encroach into the rain forest, destroying the habitat of many endangered animals.

topsoil prone to erosion, leading to mudslides, silting, and flooding. Manmade changes in the forest canopy also alter the forest climate and the growth and diversity of trees and animals. Although more than 60 percent of the country is covered in forest, only 11.6 percent can be considered pristine forest as a result of such high levels of deforestation. Ancient forest still exists in Malaysia's national park, Taman Negara, which scientists believe to be 130 million years old.

Oil-palm plantations contribute significantly to land degradation in Malaysia and are gradually taking over the rain forests. Oil palms are planted in neat rows with wide gaps in between, and rain falling on the exposed ground washes away the topsoil. Oil palms remain economically viable for 15 years on average, after which they have to be replaced. Repeated planting of oil palms depletes the soil of certain nutrients until eventually the soil loses its fertility. Apart from the depletion of the rain forest, the production of palm oil is a cause for concern because it produces a large amount of waste that damages the marine ecosystem. In 2001 the production of 7 million tons (52 million barrels) of crude palm oil generated almost 10 million tons (75 million barrels) of solid oil wastes.

ENVIRONMENTAL PROTECTION

The DOE, under the Ministry of Science, Technology, and Environment, works to fight pollution by studying the environment, monitoring sources of pollutants, educating Malaysians, and involving the people in efforts to preserve the environment. The DOE penalizes factories that discharge excessive amounts of effluents or outflow and owners of motor vehicles that emit excessive amounts of exhaust fumes, and involves nongovernmental organizations (NGOs) and the private sector in public awareness programs.

The Department of Wildlife and National Parks (DWNP) protects the flora and fauna in Peninsular Malaysia. It manages the Taman Negara National Park and the Sepilok Orangutan Sanctuary. Together with Melaka Zoo, the DWNP has carried out a successful captive breeding program for locally threatened species, including the tiger, panther, tapir, serow, barking deer, sambar deer, and many others.

The Department of Fisheries, under the Ministry of Agriculture, takes care of Malaysia's marine heritage. This department oversees the management of several marine parks, where efforts are made to protect, conserve, and manage marine ecosystems, especially coral reefs and their associated flora and fauna, for the purposes of research, education, and ecotourism. The Ma' Daerah and Rantau Abang marine reserves, operating under the fisheries department's wing, are dedicated to protecting sea turtles. The beaches of Rantau Abang are regularly visited by leatherback turtles seeking a place to lay their eggs.

Malaysia's environmental conservation efforts are having moderate success. There are stable populations of endangered animals in the national parks and wildlife sanctuaries. Keeping the environment healthy and clean has also benefitted tourism. Visitors come from all over the world to experience Malaysia's diverse culture and admire its beautiful natural environment.

INTERNET LINKS

www.doe.gov.my

The official website of the DOE provides general information, air pollution index, news and events, and much more.

www.rainforests.mongabay.com

This website is a leading source of information on tropical forests by some of the world's top ecologists and conservationists, with useful statistics on Malaysia's forests, including deforestation rates.

www.wwf.org.my/about_wwf/what_we_do/species_main/species_news

This website is instrumental in providing news gathered by the World Wildlife Fund (WWF) on Malaysia's most threatened species, such as the turtle, the orangutan, the rhinoceros, and the elephant.

MALAYSIANS

A family in a Bajao stilt house.

HISTORY AND GEOGRAPHY HAVE collaborated to make Malaysia a truly multiracial country. In the jungle areas of Borneo and the peninsula, many aboriginal peoples live in traditional ways or reluctantly adapt to life in settlements.

Starting around 4000 B.C., succeeding waves of ethnic Malays arrived from the northwest, and aboriginal peoples moved deeper into the interior of the country. Most Chinese settlement occurred in the 19th and early 20th centuries, apart from the few Chinese who landed in the 14th and 15th centuries in Melaka and later Penang.

ORANG ASLI

The aboriginal peoples of Malaysia are called Orang Asli in the peninsula. They consist of about 18 different tribal populations, numbering around 150,000 people in total, who are widely regarded as Malaysia's original inhabitants. Traditionally they lived by hunting and gathering, staying in rough shelters for a few weeks at a time and then moving on. The last generation of true nomads dates back to the Middle Ages. Many Orang Asli now live more settled lives as farmers and some even live in urban areas and work for wages. Some of the men still go off for the occasional jungle trek, but they come back to their home and families.

Indigenous peoples live in East Malaysia. In Sabah more than half the population originates from the indigenous peoples. The main indigenous groups are the Kadazandusuns. In Sarawak 50 percent of the population originates from indigenous peoples. The dominant groups include the Iban and Penan.

6

Malaysia is a melting pot of a wide variety of people of different races, beliefs, and cultures. Many now live in urban conurbations although a proportion of the population still lead rural lives.

RURAL MALAY SETTLEMENT

Many Peninsular Malays trace their origins to Sumatra, some having immigrated within the last 50 years. Borneo Malays also have Sumatran ancestors or originate from Johor. A Malay village is called a kampong, a group of single-family houses preferably built in the shelter of a river mouth. Fishing is still the main economic activity of rural Malays; fish is one of their favorite foods.

A Malay kampong typically contains its own mosque—called a *masjid* (mahs-jid)—or at least a *surau* (soo-rao)—a Muslim house of prayer. Paddy fields and Malay houses on stilts are also distinctive features of kampong. In the more populated areas of Malaysia, where people of different races live together, the Malay section of a village is often separated from the Chinese bazaar or market by a small body of water or river to make sure that no pigs (which are taboo to Muslims) invade the kampung.

LAND DEVELOPMENT PROJECTS

In rural Malaysia land development projects cover huge areas of land with oil palm, rubber, cocoa, and other cash crops. Houses for the settlers are usually provided by the developer.

Unlike in a traditional kampong, houses in a development project are uniform in design and spread out. Each unit includes a small plot of land for growing vegetables or rearing a few chickens. Houses are provided with basic sanitation, water, and electricity. There is also usually a school, a rural clinic, and a few stores.

EAST MALAYSIAN SETTLEMENTS

The longhouse is the traditional dwelling of some indigenous peoples in Sabah and Sarawak. The longhouse is a row of 12 to 50 or even more houses built side by side, so that each house shares a wall with the immediate neighbor on either side. The "village street" is a wide, covered veranda running along the front of the longhouse. Longhouses were built to protect the community. The foundation pillars rose up to 20 feet (6 m) high, and the notched log that served as a staircase was pulled up at night.

Although some people have started leaving the longhouse for kampong- or urban-style housing, many Borneans still prefer their traditional dwelling. Subsidized public housing in agricultural development areas in Sarawak may be "kampong-type" or "longhouse-type," as the settlers wish—and many Borneans prefer a modern longhouse of hewn timber, with glass windows and indoor plumbing.

A traditional East Malaysian longhouse settlement.

URBAN COMMUNITY

Malaysia is still a predominantly rural country, but the picture is changing rapidly. Kampong or longhouse people move into town for a variety of reasons. They hope to find better schools for their children and better medical and other public facilities. In addition educated young people look for employment in towns. Urban housing in Malaysia resembles that in other countries. All types of housing, including terrace, semidetached houses, and bungalows, line the roads in most towns, and modern apartments and condominiums are becoming common in the larger towns. Less planned are the squatter settlements on the urban fringes of main cities. Migrants from the villages build shacks out of readily available materials and live in their flimsy shelters temporarily—or so they hope—until they can afford proper housing.

MALAYSIAN FASHION

Because the climate is mostly hot and humid, Malaysians wear casual summer clothes all year-round. Although urban homes and offices are often air-conditioned, nobody needs sweaters. In fact cotton T-shirts and shorts

Two boys in traditional costume.

are common everyday wear for both children and adults when they are not at work or school.

When more formal dress is required, Malaysian men may wear Western-style shirts and trousers, and Malaysian women Western-style dresses, blouses, and skirts. Many dress in Western-style business suits at work. Malay women often wear modern versions of the *baju kurung* (bah-joo koo-rohng), a flowing knee-length blouse worn over an ankle-length skirt. Indian women are often seen in a gossamer sari, a 6-yard (5.5-m) length of material wrapped gracefully around the body. Their Sikh counterparts wear a *shalwar-kameez* (shehl-WAHR kheh-MEEZ), a knee-length blouse worn over baggy trousers of the same material. Sikhs are Punjabi Indians who follow the teachings of Guru Nanak, the founder of Sikhism.

Although the classical high-necked, side-slit Chinese *cheongsam* (chee-OHNG-sahm) is not much in fashion now, the *sam foo* (sahm-foo) suit of a fitted floral blouse and matching pants is still worn by some women. All Malaysian schoolchildren wear the same uniforms. For elementary school students it is white and navy. High school girls wear a white blouse and turquoise pinafore, whereas the boys wear white shirts and army-green pants. Many Muslim schoolgirls may wear a white *baju kurung* over a long turquoise skirt. The more traditional among them wrap their heads in scarves or white veils worn over tight-fitting caps. Muslim women may cover their heads with a veil, although this is not considered necessary for ordinary purposes. It is compulsory only for attending the mosque or saying prayers at home. The very orthodox follow a recently imported fashion of covering their faces in public, known as purdah. Muslim men cover their heads when engaged in devotions, wearing a rimless black hat called a *songkok* (sohng-koh), which may also be worn for everyday purposes.

Sikh boys from conservative families wear their hair uncut and formed into a tight topknot wrapped in a silk handkerchief. Their elder brothers and fathers wear the traditional turban, made up of 30 feet (9 m) of fine muslin wound over a loose-fitting cap. Sikh women wear a veil when going outdoors, but this restriction is not taken very seriously by the younger generation.

TRADITIONAL COSTUMES

Indian and Malay women often wear their traditional clothes on weekdays and to work. For holidays and festivals all Malaysians make an effort to look smart: Appearing at a festival in shabby clothes is considered disrespectful to the host and to the occasion.

Malay boys and girls are usually dressed up in miniature versions of the traditional Malay costumes worn by their parents. Chinese children may be dressed in traditional robes or trouser suits for the Chinese New Year, but this is more common for younger girls and boys.

East Malaysians bring out their festive costumes for holiday occasions. Most of these are colorful, traditional costumes combined with modern additions such as shiny satin, glittering sequins, paper flowers, and—the very latest—aluminum-foil imitations of priceless heirloom jewelry. If the real antique silver were lost or damaged, the loss could run into thousands of dollars.

INTERNET LINKS

www.malaysia-trulyasia.com /tourism/the_people.htm

This website provides a good summary of the different ethnic groups of Malaysia.

www.iwgia.org/sw18358.asp

This website provides a detailed account of the various indigenous groups that live in Malaysia, including information about lifestyle, culture, and language.

en.wikipedia.org/wiki/Demographics_of_Malaysia

This website provides a detailed analysis of the demographics of Malaysia, ranging from ethnicity, religion, language, and education, to health care.

The bustling streets of Chinatown in Kuala Lumpur.

7

> 66 A MALAYSIAN RUNS INTO A CLINIC with blood stains on his head. He inquires after the doctor's health, not forgetting grandma, grandpa, and the rest of the doctor's family. After a few remarks about the weather, he finally tells the doctor that he has had a little problem with a brick falling off a building. . . . "

This story, although exaggerated, has some truth in it. For Malaysians rules of behavior must be carefully observed within the family and one's own circle of friends.

CULTURAL NORMS

There may be personal disagreements between parents and children from time to time, but nobody seriously doubts that their elders' blessings, however formalized, are necessary for them to have "good future, prosperity, health, and long life," to quote a common Malaysian congratulatory formula.

Respect for elders and filial piety remain strong elements within Malaysian families although these values are gradually being eroded. Filial piety includes the responsibility of each person to respect their parents, obey them, take care of them as they age, advise parents, and of course, to love them.

Malay children kiss their parents' hands and beg their forgiveness on Hari Raya Puasa, which is the celebration at the end of Ramadan (the

Muslim fasting month). The practice of kissing the hands of elders is called *salam* (sah-lahm). Chinese children pay their respects to their elders on the Chinese New Year by offering them Mandarin oranges and kneeling to receive their blessings. Indian children show their obedience to their parents by allowing them to share in life's major decisions, from their choice of college to whom they may choose to marry.

Malaysians, particularly the older generation, are not prone to public displays of affection such as hugging and kissing, although generally, Malaysians are a friendly and warm people who enjoy showing hospitality to family and friends.

STRONG FAMILY TIES

Traditionally most Malaysians have lived within easy reach of their close relatives. Villagers were likely to find marriage partners within their own or a neighboring community. Any joyous or sad event is shared with a big crowd of cousins, aunts, and uncles. However small a house, there is always room for a relative to stay for a few days or a few weeks or a few years!

It is not unusual for an extended family to live together or nearby, like this family of three generations on Langkawi island.

It never fails to astonish Malaysians when foreign friends casually admit that they do not know all their own second cousins. Malaysians, whether Malay, Chinese, or Indian, usually do. Furthermore they know exactly what to call them: elder cousin, younger cousin, eldest aunt, youngest uncle. Personal names are not much used within the family context; everyone is addressed by their family "status." More traditionally minded Malaysians or those who are recent immigrants have maintained their family connections with the "old country," be it China, India, or Sumatra. For example some conservative Indian parents make sure that their children marry into a suitable family by contacting a matchmaker on the Indian subcontinent to arrange a match for a son or daughter. These arrangements do not always come to fruition and practices like this are becoming less common. Young Malaysians may have different ideas from what their parents hope for their future, although they usually feel guilty about disobeying their parents on such an important subject.

Following the formality in most Malaysian societies, it is unsurprising that even the in-law relationship is ritualized. Rudeness to the in-laws is unforgivable. Even a person who does not like his mother-in-law much would consider Western jokes on the topic in very bad taste.

BIRTH RITES AND TABOOS

Malaysians share a deep concern for their married children's and grandchildren's welfare. In particular great care is taken to protect pregnant women and newborn babies from all harm. The birthrate is 22 births for every 1,000 women.

The father-to-be has to watch his step, too. In some communities he is not allowed to kill anything, not even a snake, because it is believed that such an act would scar the unborn baby. Pregnant and newly delivered mothers keep away from the cold and wind. They do not consume "cold" foods such as vegetables, fruit, and iced drinks. Moreover, to shelter themselves from the wind, they cover their heads with a piece of cloth.

For 40 days after delivery Chinese mothers are fed chicken soup with wine and herbs in order to keep them warm. For the same number of days they cannot shampoo their hair, which can prove uncomfortable in the hot Malaysian climate. They also cannot take their newborn out, fearing the wind would harm the child.

Many modern women refuse to be hampered by such taboos, although they may pretend to go along with them so as not to offend their elders. They may put up with the soup for a week or so, then get a friend to smuggle fresh fruit into the house!

Malay babies have their heads ceremonially shaved when they are 40 days old, at the time that the mother's confinement ends. Some are also taught to

A baby should not be praised or called fat, as this may attract the attention of evil spirits. Similarly whistling in the dark will attract evil spirits.

One should not look at a baby through a mirror or the baby will drown later in life. One should not talk to a baby from the head of his cradle, as this will make him cross-eyed. Children should not sit on bed pillows or they will get boils on their buttocks. Children who are learning to write should not eat chicken feet or their handwriting will become crabbed like the scratches made by a chicken's claws.

"tread the ground" at this age. Since they are still far too young to walk, their tiny feet are brushed gently against the ground, or a handful of earth is held against the soles of their feet.

GROWING UP IN MALAYSIA

In the past children in rural Malaysia who lived in kampongs and longhouses enjoyed an idyllic and carefree childhood. The children who lived in towns may have had less freedom—for example Chinese children may have been expected to help out in their family-run shop from an early age. A Malay or Dayak boy can play by the water with his friends and run home for a snack or a nap when it suits him, while his sister helps their mother with household chores. He may go fishing and add his catch to the family meal, but nobody tells him to do so.

Malaysian children are very much included in adult social life. At all-night parties or ceremonies, children are often found observing the proceedings or dropping off to sleep in a corner.

At the age of 5 or 6, Malay boys are sent to a Koran teacher to learn Muslim scripture. They have to master Arabic writing, then words and sentences, then whole chapters of the holy book. Malay girls, too, are proficient in the art of Koran reading. The boys cover their head with a *songkok*; the girls wear a muslin veil when handling or reading the Koran.

A party is held when a boy has finished studying the holy book. Dressed in his best clothes and supervised by his proud teachers and parents, he has to give a public recital of his accomplishment.

At the age of 10 to 12, after they have completed reading the Koran, Malay boys are circumcised as their religion demands. Circumcision used to be a semipublic event that involved a feast for the whole kampong. Nowadays the minor operation is performed by a doctor, in the privacy of a clinic or hospital. The family may give a meal to celebrate the safe completion of this rite, inviting only close relatives.

Students in class at an Islamic school in Kuching.

In the past some girls were circumcised, too, but not in the drastic fashion that is prevalent in some parts of Africa. A slight nick, usually administered by the child's mother or the village midwife, satisfies the demands of Muslim tradition.

GOING TO SCHOOL

Malaysian children from the ages of 6 to 16 enjoy free compulsory education. Children begin elementary school at the age of 6 in classes that are fairly large and strictly disciplined. Each child sits at his or her desk during normal lesson time and has to learn a lot of material by heart.

Attendance is well over 90 percent at elementary school and over 80 percent at secondary school. Children spend an average of 13 years in education from elementary to tertiary level.

The literacy rate in Malaysia is 93.5 percent. The Malaysian government gives high priority to education, spending 6.2 percent of its GDP on education. Available places in institutions of higher learning—including about 10 universities—are limited and competition is stiff.

A Malaysian woman working at a factory. The number of women joining the workforce is increasing.

Malaysian schoolchildren wear uniforms. Girls are not allowed to wear jewelry, makeup, colorful socks and shoes, or hair ribbons in any color other than their uniform colors. Boys must keep their hair short. If their hair is long enough to touch the top of their shirt collar at the back, they may face disciplinary action.

In most Malaysian schools students have to stand up when they answer a question. When a teacher enters the classroom, the students rise and greet the teacher in chorus, saying, "*Selamat pagi, cikgu*" (Seh-lah-maht pah-gi, cheh-goo), meaning "Good morning, teacher." In rural areas secondary schools have large boarding houses for students who live far away. They only go home for holidays.

THE ROLE OF WOMEN

Within most ordinary Malaysian households, the wife and mother reigns supreme. Although the father is acknowledged as the head of the family, few would dispute the woman's important role within a Malaysian home.

Many women and mothers in Malaysian today work outside the home as well as manage the house and the lives of her family members. She may have an equal say in exactly what proportion of the family's income will be spent on education, what the best school and career is for each of her children, and where to invest the family's savings. And she is likely to play a large part in her grown-up children's marriage plans.

Malaysian women are slowly making an impact on the young country's public life, either in government or in the business world. Although women make up approximately half the population, they represent only a third of the actual workforce. Many women who do work tend to be casual laborers who earn low salaries doing work such as cleaning, cooking, or serving at small food stalls.

There is a growing sector of professional women, but as in many Asian countries, they face discrimination, particularly in the form of unequal pay. Many women find that they are passed over for promotions and their needs at work are overlooked.

In Malaysian political life only 14 percent of the Cabinet members are women—there are 10 women ministers and deputy ministers out of a total of 71 serving in the Cabinet. The Ministry of Women, Family and Community Development is focused on improving the status of all women in Malaysia.

The life expectancy of a Malaysian woman is 76 years, compared with 71 years for a Malaysian man.

COURTSHIP

In Malaysia a person at age 21 is free to choose his or her marriage partner. How do Malaysians find their future spouses? By the time Malaysian teenagers enter college, some may have paired up and are beginning to think about marriage and starting their own families. Living together without getting married first is rare in Malaysia, and having children out of wedlock is generally disapproved of within the community.

What is considered acceptable dating behavior in towns may be objectionable in the eyes of country folk. Generally kissing in public is frowned upon. In cities and towns it is common to see young couples walking hand-in-hand. However, in more rural areas, particularly where the people are predominantly Muslim, emotional displays of affection are considered too explicit and may be illegal under Islamic law. For example, in the town of Kota Bahru on the east coast of Malaysia, rules of behavior between members of the opposite sex have to follow the strict laws of Islam. The Islamic law of *khalwat* is used to ensure that men and women do not come into close proximity with each other until they are married. As a result separate checkout counters exist in supermarkets. There are also strict rules that discourage Muslim women from dressing indecently. Indecent dress would include short skirts and figure-hugging clothing that reveals parts of the body.

A Malay couple in traditional wedding clothing.

Indian families tend to be heavily involved in looking for spouses for their children. A matchmaker, considering the history and the social and economic position of the family, draws up horoscopes of possible partners. In the past many happily married middle-aged Indian couples never met before their wedding day! A bride is expected to be a virgin; conservative in-laws may make her life unpleasant if she is not.

MARRIAGE

The different ethnic groups in Malaysia celebrate weddings according to their own customs. Even among people of the same race and religion, marriage ceremonies may vary from region to region. Weddings today, irrespective of ethnic group, contain both traditional and modern elements. Many couples choose to have the actual wedding ceremony at home or in a religious venue such as a temple, church, or mosque. However, wedding receptions are usually held in large restaurants or luxury hotels. Generally Malaysians enjoy weddings, and they are large, colorful, noisy, and fun-filled affairs. Those described here are the most common in Malaysia.

MALAY WEDDINGS Even if a young man has chosen his future wife, his parents have to "obtain" his bride for him. Senior relatives visit the woman's house to inquire whether the young lady is available for marriage (meaning unbetrothed). If the reply is encouraging both sides fix an auspicious day for the betrothal and agree on the dowry and share of expenses. Other gift items exchanged may include a ring, a complete trousseau, good-quality cloth (such as silk), a complete betel-nut set, cakes, and fruit.

REGIONAL MALAY WEDDING CUSTOMS

The engagement ring is placed on the fourth finger of the bride's right hand by a senior female relative of the groom.

A few weeks before the wedding the accepted suitor spends a night at his bride-to-be's home. After he has left the bride-to-be and her sisters search for gifts of gold hidden in the bedding of the room in which he slept.

The day before the wedding bride and groom have their hands and feet stained red with henna. The bride's hair is trimmed by an elderly female attendant called Mak Andam.

The bridegroom is denied entry into the bride's house by a champion. A member of his entourage has to "fight" his way up the steps. The best man "bribes" the women of the household to permit the groom access to the inner rooms.

After the bersanding *ceremony, the bride and groom have to feed one another morsels of sweetened rice. This is hilariously messy, but with Mak Andam's help they manage and the wedding feast can begin.*

The morning after the wedding, the couple is made to sit on the back steps. Water is poured over them through a cloth. In the southern state of Johor this leads to a free-for-all splashing party.

The woman is then informed by her mother that she is to become a bride. It is customary that she act surprised even if the man is her heart's choice. On the other hand few Malay women nowadays would marry a man they do not like just because their parents have accepted him. Most parents have also adapted to the younger generation's ways by consulting their child before a response is returned. The engagement may be held several months before the wedding, or on the day before the ceremony. It is announced to make a family agreement public.

Malay weddings may last several days and follow Muslim laws and customs. The essential part of a Muslim marriage is the *nikah* ceremony where the marriage contract is signed and includes the bridegroom's declaration to his new father-in-law that he will provide for his wife and treat

A Chinese couple offering tea to the elders in their families during the traditional tea ceremony.

her well. This is done before mosque officials and other witnesses. After the groom has done so to everyone's satisfaction—he may be required to repeat it if it was not loud enough—he is led to *bersanding*, or "sit in state," beside his bride.

CHINESE WEDDINGS The splendid old-fashioned wedding ceremonies of the Malaysian Chinese are the subject of museum exhibits today. Malaysian Chinese who are Christians marry in a church. Others opt for marriage at the clan temple or the registry office.

One tradition still observed is the "engagement sweet." The girl's parents order large quantities of a special sweet that is wrapped in red paper and labeled with the engaged couple's names. This is then sent to all relatives and friends to announce the forthcoming wedding.

The color red—in the form of red paper, red banners, and red decorations—plays a prominent part in all Chinese weddings, whether they are traditional, church, or registry. The invitations are printed on red cards, and guests bring a present of money in a red envelope. Red signifies luck.

Even modern families observe some old-fashioned customs, the most important one being the tea ceremony in which the bride offers tea to her parents-in-law. Acceptance of the tea offered demonstrates acceptance of the daughter-in-law into the family.

Other customs are observed simply for fun. One such tradition is that only the bride's younger brother can open the groom's car door. When the groom arrives the boy cannot be found and has to be noisily searched for. Then he proves to be clumsy with the door handle. A large "bribe," usually a sum of money wrapped in red paper, suddenly improves his skills, and he then lets his future elder brother-in-law out of the car with many respectful bows.

HINDU WEDDINGS Traditionally the first time a Hindu couple met was at their wedding. Modern Hindu couples are more likely to have established a relationship before the wedding.

Three essential ceremonies mark a Hindu wedding: The married women of the family plant a sacred pipal (fig) tree for the couple; the father of the bride gives his daughter away by putting her hand in the bridegroom's; and instead of a wedding ring, the bridegroom fixes a gold *thali* (taah-li), or pendant, around the bride's neck as a sign that she is legally his wife. The newly married couple then paces seven times around a flame that is sacred to the fire god Agni. The bride's veil is tied to the groom's sash to symbolize that "the knot has been tied." The officiating priest throws butter, rice, and flowers into the fire.

The morning after the wedding the young husband stains the part in his wife's hair with vermilion powder, symbolizing her new status. From now on, the young wife wears gold earrings, necklaces, bangles, and rings, as befits a married woman—only a widow goes unadorned.

A Hindu wedding ceremony is a colorful and elaborate affair.

SIKH WEDDINGS In the past the Sikh bride was wrapped in a long white cloth and carried to the groom by her brothers. The modern Sikh bride walks on her own, suitably escorted. She wears a veil and a red and gold *shalwar-kameez*, the traditional dress for Sikh women. Her groom is likely to wear a Western-style suit or he may be dressed in traditional shirt and trousers with a red or dark pink turban and a colored scarf.

The Sikh religious wedding ceremony, known as *Anand Karaj* or "Blissful Union," takes place in a Sikh temple. The Sikh marriage represents the union of two individuals as equals. The newly married Sikh couple vows to help one another toward their goal of merging both their souls with God. The bride and groom, surrounded by family and friends, take their vows in front of the Sikh holy book, the *Adi Granth*. To conclude the ceremony, the groom leads the bride four times around the Adi Granth.

WORKING LIFE

Most young Malaysians start looking for jobs after 9 to 13 years of formal education. Young Malaysians entering the workforce tend to prefer jobs in the government or private sector, and many set up their own businesses or help run established family businesses. It is increasingly hard to find young Malaysians who are willing to take on jobs in the rural areas such as fishing or agriculture. Out of more than 11 million workers, 57 percent are employed in the services industry, 28 percent in industry, and 15 percent in agriculture.

Young Malaysian women usually keep their jobs after marriage. Once babies arrive, however, the working mother has to decide whether to continue working and rely on a relative or a paid housemaid to look after the children or to give up her job and stay home to take care of the little ones.

Many Malaysian couples can count on a grandmother, aunt, or some other relative to help watch their baby when they go out to work. In many households the housemaid becomes an important family member, taking the place of the mother. For couples who are not blessed with family members who can take care of their children and who cannot afford to pay a maid, the wife may have to stay home. Day-care facilities at the workplace are not common, and it is almost unheard of for fathers to give up their jobs and stay at home with the children.

Like people of many other countries around the world, Malaysians are looking for more flexible working hours so they can achieve a better work-life balance.

POVERTY

In 2002 official figures indicated that 5.1 percent of the population live below the poverty line. The number of poor households was calculated to be 257,900 in 2002. Poverty in Malaysia is set at RM500 ringgit or US$160 per month for a family of four. Real average per capita income was US$13,800 in 2009.

Although Malaysia has been quite successful in alleviating poverty, pockets of poverty still exist, typically in the rural areas. The most impoverished groups are the farmers and fishermen. However, because most of them get some of their daily sustenance directly from their work, their situation may not be as bad as the numbers suggest. Urban poverty is becoming more of a problem since a large proportion of the population has moved from rural to urban areas within the last three decades. Migration to urban centers increased from 27 percent in 1970 to a staggering 51 percent in 2007.

Poverty in the towns is manifested in street beggars, many of whom are handicapped. Blind beggars near the entrance of a mosque hope to receive alms from the faithful as they enter to pray. If they do not cause trouble, beggars are tolerated. An exception is child beggars, forced to beg by their "owners," who may have bought them from their parents. Such children are placed in orphanages by welfare authorities. Urban poverty is also evident in squatter settlements that dot the outskirts of major towns and cities, although the authorities have eradicated some of these successfully.

About a third of government budget has been devoted to the provision of social services, including education and health care. The government is also focusing efforts on providing the very poor with subsidized or free housing and food and small grants and agriculture extension programs to support their income. Needy children are put into nutritional programs, awarded scholarships, and given free textbooks.

DEATH RITES

When someone dies, as many family members as possible congregate in the home of the bereaved. Since the hot and humid climate requires the quick burial or cremation of the dead, not everyone is able to make it to the funeral in time. Many cultures observe rites on certain days after the funeral so that those who could not attend the funeral are able to pay their respects.

A Chinese tombstone.

MUSLIM Muslims immediately inform the local mosque officials when somebody has passed away. The body is washed and shrouded. Only the face is left free and is covered with a fine muslin cloth, which relatives may reverently lift for one last look. Until the funeral, which usually takes place before sunset on the same day, family and friends keep vigil.

Before burial the body is fully shrouded, placed on a bier or in a coffin, and taken to the cemetery. Family members would have dug the grave by then. The body is taken out of the coffin and gently placed in the earth. The call to prayer is recited in the deceased's ear, after which the grave is filled in.

A religious official, protected by an umbrella, recites prayers over the new grave. Flowers, sandalwood shavings, and water are strewn over the raw earth. Only men are allowed to attend the burial.

Orthodox Islam discourages people from erecting tombstones and elaborate markers, or putting flowers or other mementos at the gravesite.

CHINESE Wealthy Chinese spend a lot of money on a "respectable" funeral. Economy at such a time would be severely criticized by relatives and friends.

A traditional Chinese coffin is hewn out of the trunk of one hardwood tree, a very expensive receptacle. The body is wrapped in many layers of silk gauze and placed in the coffin. Once the heavy coffin is sealed, it may be kept in the house or funeral parlor for several days until all the preparations are ready.

Buddhist monks are invited to chant hymns, and members of the deceased's clan association or family serve tea to mourners, keep a record of gifts presented, and generally act as undertakers.

The funeral procession leaves at a predetermined time, often 2:00 P.M. Direct descendants are dressed in shapeless garments of unbleached calico or indigo cotton. The cortege is supposed to walk to the burial site (although cremation is becoming common). If the site is more than a mile (1.6 km) away, the bereaved family arranges for buses to send the mourners from a certain point along the route.

At the cemetery the bereaved family presents each person with a new handkerchief that has a red thread sewn into one of the corners. Upon leaving the graveyard this cloth should be waved over one shoulder so that spirits cannot follow the mourners.

INDIAN Sikhs and some non-Muslim Indians cremate their dead. This used to be done on an open-air funeral pyre, where tradition demanded that the deceased's son or other close male relative light the fire. Modern crematoria are now available in Malaysia's main towns.

INTERNET LINKS

www.myworklife.my

This website is a platform dedicated to providing relevant information for returning Malaysians or foreigners who are interested in working. It also serves as the preferred source of information on government-linked companies as well as the broader Malaysian environment.

www.kwintessential.co.uk/resources/global-etiquette/malaysia.html

This website is a guide to Malaysia's culture, customs, etiquette, and languages, including appropriate ways to meet and greet, understanding Malaysian names, gift-giving customs, business etiquette and protocol, and more.

www.tourism.gov.my

This official portal of Malaysia provides information on Malaysia's rich culture and heritage. This website also offers an in-depth guide about things to do and see in and around Malaysia, including featured destinations and special events.

RELIGION

Ubudiah Mosque in Kuala Kangsar, Perak.
Islam being the national religion means that
mosques are common sights in Malaysia.

8

MALAYSIA IS A LAND OF DIVERSE faiths. The 2000 census states that Muslims make up the largest group—60.4 percent of the population.

Malaysian Buddhists are mainly from the Chinese ethnic group and they constitute 19.2 percent, with 2.6 percent following Confucianism, Taoism (also known as Daoism), and other traditional Chinese religions. Christians represent 9.1 percent, Hindus 6.3 percent and 2.4 percent adhering to other beliefs or none at all. Hinduism, Buddhism, and Islam reached Malaysia from India and China. In the early days of the Melaka kingdom, the court was influenced by Indian Hindu beliefs. Islam is generally thought to have arrived in Melaka in the 15th century, although recent discoveries may push that date back significantly.

The first Christian church in Malaysia was built by the Portuguese in Melaka. More Christian missionaries arrived in the late 19th century. They never attempted to convert the Muslims, devoting their labors to converting the "pagans" instead.

The country's oldest indigenous religion is animism, where the object of worship is nature. The devoted believe that animals, plants, and natural phenomena such as the weather are imbued with spirits. The indigenous tribes of Peninsular Malaysia—the Orang Asli—and some tribal groups in Borneo are animists, or were so until quite recently.

ISLAM

According to the Malaysian Constitution, Malays are legally defined as Muslims and follow the Islamic faith. Islam is a Middle Eastern religion based on the revelations of the Prophet Muhammad in the seventh century A.D.

Islam is the official religion of Malaysia, mainly practiced by the Malays. The non-Malays mainly follow the religions of Taoism, Buddhism, Christianity, and Hinduism.

Muslims are obliged to profess their faith, pray five times a day, pay a tithe of their income to the mosque, fast during the month of Ramadan, and make a pilgrimage to Mecca once in their lifetime. The earliest prayer, *subuh* (soo-BUH), is said from about 5:45 A.M. to 6:00 A.M. to coincide with the first blush of dawn. The *zuhur* (zoo-HUR) hour is at noon, *asar* (AH-sar) at 4:00 P.M., *mahgrib* (MAH-grib) at dusk, and *isyak* (EE-shah) after dark. Not every Muslim observes all the hours of prayer, but the call to prayer is heard from the towers of mosques. Sung by a gifted cantor in the old days, the prayers today are recordings that are replayed and amplified.

Muslims wash their face, hands, and feet before prayer, and put on special clothes. Men wear long sleeves, long trousers, or a cotton *sarung* (SAH-rohng). They cover their heads with a rimless black hat called a *songkok* or, if they have performed the pilgrimage, a flat white cap. Women drape a voluminous garment around themselves to go to the mosque or when praying at home.

One month of the Muslim calendar is devoted to fasting, or *puasa* (poo-ah-sah). During this month, known as Ramadan, no food or water may be consumed from before dawn until after dark. Night is turned into day with a "breakfast" after the evening prayer, a dinner at midnight, and a sustaining predawn meal before *subuh* prayers.

Muslims at Friday prayers at the Masjid Kampung Mosque.

In the past the pilgrimage to Mecca was a momentous undertaking. Not many men, and very few women, ever saw the holy places. Today the Malaysian government encourages Muslims to undertake the pilgrimage. Through a savings plan, people can accumulate the necessary funds.

The Pilgrimage Fund Board, called Tabung Haji, provides help in arranging this important religious trip for them.

HINDUISM

Hinduism is one of the oldest living religions, dating to prehistoric times in India. Hindus revere a pantheon of gods, led by the Lord Shiva, who rides on a bull, and his consort Durga, who is usually portrayed astride a tiger. The august couple symbolizes creation, preservation, and destruction. The main feature of the Hindu religion is that there is no compulsion to do a certain thing. Pious Hindus have a little shrine in the house where lamps are lit and offerings of flowers and fruit are made daily, but no divine wrath threatens if this ritual is omitted. People go to the temple when it suits them, not because it is the holy day of the week.

By living a good life Hindus can ensure that they will be reincarnated as a good person in their next life. A miscreant may be reborn as a low animal or an insect. Hindus sometimes consult an elaborate horoscope before making important decisions. A religious man interprets it for them.

Malaysian Indians celebrate a number of festivals, among them Deepavali, also known as the festival of lights. This Hindu festival of lights symbolizes the triumph of good over evil. It is observed by Hindus of all sects. The family cleans the house and puts on their best clothes. They decorate the house and garden with candles and oil lamps that twinkle at dusk. Deepavali marks the end of the business year for some communities.

The Hindu temple, Sri Mahamariamma, in Kuala Lumpur.

TAOISM, CONFUCIANISM, AND BUDDHISM

Most Chinese in Malaysia would say simply that they are "Buddhists," although in reality, many practice a mixture of Buddhism, Taoism, and Confucianism. The picturesque Chinese temples in the country house figurines of many different Chinese gods and often a statue of the Buddha as well. However, these temples are not strictly Buddhist.

Buddhism and Confucianism are said to appeal to the intellect, while a popular version of Taoism is considered the religion of the masses. Taoism venerates a multitude of gods and includes the worship of ancestors. Regional and local gods, deified heroes, and ancestors have a place in the Chinese temple. The Chinese who migrated to Malaysia over the centuries brought along their own gods and immortals. In the past the village temple was often the site of the school, and the temple committee was also functioning as the school committee.

Worshipers at the Taoist Sze Ya Temple, the oldest temple in Chinatown, Kuala Lumpur.

Temple festivals follow the Chinese lunar calendar. The beginning of the new moon is celebrated by lighting incense sticks (known as joss sticks) or burning "hell money" in big-bellied incinerators. *Hell money* is the term for banknotes of huge denominations (not real, of course), sold for a few dollars per bundle, that humans use to pay celestial debts. The main Buddhist festival is Wesak, which is a celebration to commemorate the birth of the Buddha. Famous temples in Malaysia include the Snake Temple, Kek Lok Si, and Khoo Kongsi in Penang, Cheng Hoon Teng in Melaka, and Maha Vihara and Thean Hou Temple in Kuala Lumpur.

CHRISTIANITY

The first Christian churches in Malaysia were built in Melaka after 1511 by the Portuguese. In 1553 the remains of Saint Francis Xavier were buried temporarily in the cathedral at Melaka until a permanent resting place was found in Goa in India.

The Portuguese cathedral suffered the fate of many pioneering religious edifices. When the Dutch took control of Melaka in 1641, they converted the cathedral to a Protestant church and renamed it Saint Paul's Cathedral. The Dutch also added Christ Church to the town's landscape. This blood-red building, constructed in the Northern Renaissance style, can still be visited today.

Christ Church in Melaka is part of the legacy left behind by the Dutch.

Christian churches were constructed in Penang, too, and later in Singapore. These churches mostly served the foreign trading community. The Malay inhabitants of the peninsula remained Muslims.

In the early 19th century there was considerable Christian missionary activity in Sarawak and North Borneo (Sabah). The missionaries usually left the Muslims on the peninsula alone and concentrated on the animist tribes. This practice is still prevalent today where Christian missionaries refrain from evangelizing to the Muslim community. Today both Sabah and Sarawak have the highest numbers of Christians throughout Malaysia.

The present clerical members of the various churches in Malaysia are rarely foreigners. The bishops, priests, pastors, moderators, officers, and presidents of the Catholic, Anglican, and major Protestant churches in Malaysia are now mostly local. Malaysian Christians celebrate major Christian festivals, including Christmas, Easter, and Good Friday.

WHY THE IBAN OF SARAWAK LISTEN TO OMEN BIRDS

(as told by Manang Jabing of Rimbas)

We Iban are not as ignorant as you may think. We, too, had writing once upon a time, but it was lost.

Long, long ago there was a huge flood. All the world's people had to run and swim for it. The European put a page of his writing into his hat. The Chinese stuffed a sheet of his letters into the breast pocket of his shirt. But our ancestor had neither hat nor shirt, so he put his writing into the back of his loincloth and swam for his life.

Later they met on high land. The European took the paper out of his hat. It was dry, and everybody could read it. The Chinese took the paper out of his pocket. It had got wet and the ink was running. That's why Chinese writing looks so squiggly and nobody else can read it.

The Iban took his paper out of his waistband. It was wet, too, so he spread it out on a low bush to dry. Then he went off to the jungle to do a little hunting; the flood had made him hungry.

When he came back to retrieve his writing, the sheet was gone. Birds had eaten it.

The birds have eaten all our ancestors' wisdom. No wonder the birds are so wise. If we want to know when to start a farm, to build a house, to go hunting or fishing, we ask the birds. They've got the writing—they can tell us.

ANIMISM

To an animist all of nature is God. Most animists are jungle dwellers, exposed to climatic dangers and accidents that they hardly understand. Various spirits reside in various plants and animals. An insect calling from under the house may be a messenger from the underworld. A python crawling into a jungle shelter of an Orang Asli or person from Malaysia's indigenous tribe, may be the personification of a recently deceased family member and should therefore not be chased away. (Fortunately the python is not a poisonous snake.) Each tree, each plant, each animal, and each sound has spiritual meaning, and the anger of any one of the many spirits brings bad luck.

Responsibility for bad luck is thus often conveniently shifted from humans to the spirits. A farmer who hurts himself with his ax while felling trees is not careless or clumsy; he must have unknowingly offended one of the thousands of minor forest deities or forgotten some part of a taboo or ritual. His wound is just as painful, but the mishap is not directly his fault.

Animists in the Malay Peninsula and Borneo worship large trees, but their farming method forces them to clear parts of the jungle every year. They never fell a tree without first performing elaborate rituals to inform the wood spirits. An offering is placed on the stump of the first tree felled.

Some animist tribes never clear jungles, build houses, or do any form of communal work without first consulting the spirits of the jungle, which they believe are embodied in omen birds.

SUPERSTITIONS

Chinese-speaking Malaysians have many superstitions regarding numbers. Depending on the dialect and therefore the pronunciation, a number may mean something important or dreadful. For instance the number 8 sounds like "prosperity" in Mandarin and Cantonese, making August 8, 1988 (or 8-8-88) one of the luckiest days of the 20th century. Confident of conjugal bliss, droves of couples married on that date. It is too soon to say whether they all lived happily ever after!

September 9, 1999, was a similarly auspicious date for Malaysian couples. That day nearly three times more couples registered to marry than usual.

For Hokkien speakers the number 4 is pronounced like the word for "death," *si*. Car owners are likely to object if their license plate contains such an unlucky digit. In this view one can well imagine the anger of a Penang gentleman who was given the license plate number "PAK-4." Pronounced *pak si* (pahk-SEE), this roughly means "drop dead."

Many superstitions relate to birth and death. Pregnant women are not allowed to attend funerals, and they are carefully protected from ghosts and vampires. Few Malaysians go to a graveyard without good reason. The Chinese are known to visit graveyards in the dead of night bearing offerings

(according to the Chinese horoscope)

Symbol	Year	May marry	Year	May not marry	Year
Ox	1985	Snake	1989	Tiger	1986
	1997		2001		1998
		Rat	1984	Goat	1979
			1996		1991
Monkey	1980	Dragon	1988	Ox	1985
	1992		2000		1997
		Rat	1984	Tiger	1986
			1996		1998
Rabbit	1987	Pig	1983	Rooster	1981
	1999		1995		1993
		Dog	1982	Rat	1984
			1994		1996

in the hope of receiving lucky lottery numbers from dead relatives. A body kept in the house prior to burial is carefully watched—it is believed that if a cat happens to jump over the coffin, the corpse will become a ghoul.

Abandoned houses, dark trees, and tombs are thought to be haunted. The two rules of thumb regarding these are: Keep away from such places or approach them and wrest a lucky omen from the resident ghost.

STRONG FOLK BELIEF IN MAGIC

When asked, most educated Malaysians insist that they are not superstitious. Yet magicians, mediums, witch doctors, and faith healers of all kinds enjoy good business in Malaysia.

There is a general belief that although the doctor at the local hospital (who is usually Western-trained) may be a very good person, he or she can only deal with naturally caused sickness. Penicillin is not much use against an enemy's wicked spells. Only a spell more wicked than the original one will deal with that sort of complaint. At times like that a Malaysian may consult a Malay magician or a *bomoh* (boh-MOH).

A *bomoh* is a shaman in Malaysia, known for his healing powers, protective magic, and knowledge of medicinal herbs. Because of Islamic disapproval of black magic, *bomohs* have become increasingly unpopular since the 1970s. In spite of this some people still use the services of the *bomoh*, while others have become more suspicious of their capabilities. In the past certain states retained the services of a *bomoh* to ensure good weather during open-air festivities.

Many kampong sports teams employ magic to help them win. A *bomoh* blows holy smoke over the team's soccer boots or equips them with amulets. If he can get to the field before the match (the home team will guard against such an occurrence), he plants a little charm near the goalposts.

Many children wear magic safeguards in the form of silver capsules, sacred threads, or rattan bracelets. A cross on a little chain is not just a symbol of the wearer's religion but a talisman to ward off evil. Non-Christians may sneak into a Catholic church to "borrow" some of the holy water there.

Some magicians perform black magic to inflict damage. Evil spirits are called to the magician's aid. A really bad magician tells an egg to undermine a certain person's health, slowly rot his flesh, and dissolve his very bones. The victim must find a more powerful *bomoh* to defuse the spell and send out a stronger one against the instigator. And so it goes, like the escalation of an arms race.

ASTROLOGY AND SOOTHSAYING

Some Malaysians, especially members of the older generation, believe in the powers of astrologers and soothsayers. Some important statesmen and powerful businessmen even have their own personal astrologers. It is understood that a sensible man needs more than human guidance to make important decisions.

When a baby is born, especially the first son, Hindu families may ask an astrologer to cast a horoscope for the child's entire life. The very minute of the infant's birth has to be determined, and from there his life will be charted by the stars.

The Chinese zodiac has a 12-year cycle, with each year guarded by an animal, such as a pig, rabbit, or tiger. Each animal represents certain personality traits, and a person born in the year of that animal is believed to assume some of the animal's traits.

Malaysians generally like to peer into the future by means other than horoscopes too. One can consult a professional fortune-teller, who may have a nameplate outside his door reading *Tukang Ramal* (too-KANG RAH-mahl), meaning "future maker." He uses various methods; palm reading is fairly widespread, but is not the only technique.

A fortune-teller in George Town, Penang.

Some fortune-tellers keep a tame animal such as a mouse or hamster. Strips of paper are put into its cage for it to tear into shreds. The client's fortune is then predicted from the scraps that fall outside the cage.

Many Chinese temples employ mediums who can work themselves into a trance and tell fortunes by uttering cryptic remarks that must be interpreted by a competent attendant.

The do-it-yourself method is to borrow a bamboo quiver full of long wooden or ivory sticks from the temple guardian. The devotee, having offered prayers, incense, and suitable gifts, shakes the quiver until one or several sticks fall out. The future is deciphered by interpreting the inscriptions on the various sticks.

Unlike their counterparts at carnivals in the West, fortune-tellers and astrologers are respected members of the Malaysian community. Although orthodox religions like Islam and Christianity are not entirely at ease with these practices, the general public patronizes astrologers in large numbers.

INTERNET LINKS

www.asia-planet.net/malaysia/religion.htm

This website provides a brief overview on the dominant religions practiced in Malaysia, including Islam, the Chinese religions, Hinduism, Sikhism, and Christianity.

www.asianinfo.org/asianinfo/culture_society/religion/malaysia.htm

This website serves as a guide to the main religions of Malaysia—Islam, Buddhism, Christianity, and other smaller religions. It also provides links to useful websites of associations, groups, and centers connected to the various religions.

www.islamcan.com/islamic-history/islam-in-malaysia.shtml

This website provides a summary of the history of Islam in Malaysia with a focus on the spread of Islam throughout the country.

LANGUAGE

In a multicultural society like Malaysia's, newspapers in different languages are readily available.

9

Malaysia is a
multilingual
country. Many of
its people are at
least bilingual
and can speak a
combination of
Malay, English,
as well as the
many Chinese and
Indian dialects.

THE OFFICIAL LANGUAGE OF Malaysia is Bahasa Malaysia, a standardized form of Malay. *Bahasa* (bah-hah-sah) means "language." Malay has long been the lingua franca of the Malay archipelago. Natives and traders from Sumatra to the Philippines and those living in the coastal areas of Borneo and New Guinea can often speak some form of Malay.

MULTILINGUALISM

The official language is not the only language, of course. Chinese is spoken by Malaysia's second-largest ethnic group: some 6.1 million Chinese. However, they may not necessarily understand one another, because the various Chinese languages and dialects—Mandarin, Hokkien, Hakka, Cantonese, Hainanese, and Teochew—may be mutually unintelligible. A Malaysian Chinese may speak to another in a Chinese dialect, Malay, or even English.

The 1.8 million Indians in Malaysia are also divided into linguistic units: Tamil, Telugu, Punjabi, Hindi, Gujarati, and Urdu. East Malaysia is the land of the "small" languages—some used by just a few thousand people—because rugged terrain and intertribal warfare have isolated people from one another. Some Sarawak languages are Iban, Bidayuh, Melanau, Kayan, Kenyah, Kelabit, and Lun Dayeh. In Sabah one might hear Rungus, Murut, Bisaya, Bajau, Illanun, and Suluk. The main East Malaysian indigenous languages are Iban and Kadazan.

MALAYSIAN ENGLISH

Because of the many languages spoken by the different ethnic groups in Malaysia, a unique version of English has developed over the decades, affectionately known as Malaysian English. Malaysian English is broadly based on British English but is mixed with words from the Malay, Chinese, and Indian languages. In addition to the blending of vocabulary from the local languages and dialects, Malaysian English has its own special syntax, grammar, and intonations, which it has borrowed from local dialects such as Hokkien or Tamil. Although there is no official recognition that Malaysian English exists, it is evident that when listening to Malaysians speak English to one another they speak Malaysian English, especially in social situations to friends and family.

Those exposed to Malaysian English will be familiar with the word *lah* that is used at the end of a sentence, usually as an exclamation or to affirm a statement. For example Malaysians will often say "No, lah!" when denying something categorically. Similarly "Die, lah" is used when someone wants to express that he is in trouble. Other common words that are used in Malaysian English include the Malay expression *Alamak* or the Chinese word *Aiyoh*, which both mean "Oh, no!" For instance a Malaysian who is in a hurry may say "Alamak! I'm late!"

NEWSPAPERS IN MALAYSIA

Newspapers in Malaysia come in a variety of languages, including Bahasa Malaysia, English, a few Chinese and Indian languages, and Kadazan. The majority of these newspapers are printed in roman script, but some languages have their own scripts.

There are more than 30 newspapers and tabloids published today that include *The Star*, *New Straits Times*, *The Sun*, *Berita Harian*, *Utusan Malaysia*, *Sin Chew Jit Poh*, and *Nanyang Siang Pau*.

Malay has no script of its own. Islamic missionaries brought with them the Koran and a system of writing that could be used to transcribe Malay quite accurately. The Arabic script, known as *jawi* (jah-wee) in Malaysia, is still used for some religious and formal purposes.

When Europeans first began to travel and trade in the region, they recorded names and technical terms that interested them in a rough and ready fashion. Depending on whether the scribe was Portuguese, Dutch, or English, he would write *Suraia*, *Soeraja*, or *Sooraya* for the same name. Over the years a generally accepted romanized system of written Malay has crystallized. Malay newspapers are printed either in jawi or in romanized Malay.

Chinese languages like Mandarin are written in ideograms. Each character stands for an idea or a combination of ideas. A "simplified" version of written Chinese—used in newspapers, among other things—contains 2,500 to 3,000 characters.

Indian language newspapers are printed in the specific scripts of Tamil, Punjabi, Urdu, and Malayalam. However, these languages can be rendered in roman script for other purposes.

A trishaw rider reads the newspapers while taking a break.

BAHASA MALAYSIA

Bahasa Malaysia is, in a way, a synthetic language. It is a standardized form of the dialect variants of the Malay language. Schoolchildren occasionally have difficulty distinguishing between "proper" language and the form they speak at home. The two are nearly the same, but not quite. Some non-Malays speak an imperfect form of Bahasa Malaysia called *Bahasa Pasar* (pah-sahr), which literally means "language of the marketplace."

Most Malaysians are bilingual and many are multilingual. Apart from

Here are a few simple phrases in Bahasa Malaysia that you can try.
Pronounce the vowels as follows: a as in "father," e as in "pet," i as in "pit," o as in "pot," and u as in "put."

Good morning!	Selamat pagi!
How are you?	Apa khabar?
Fine, thank you.	Baik, terima kasih.
What's your name?	Siapa nama anda?
My name is Ben.	Nama saya Ben.
Malaysia is hot, but it rains a lot.	Negeri Malaysia panas tetapi selalu hujan.
Come with me!	Mari ikut saya!
My father's house is not very big.	Rumah ayah saya tidak berapa besar.
Come up the stairs to the house!	Sila naik tangga ke rumah!
Only my little sister was at home; my parents were at work.	Hanya adik saya berada di rumah; ibu dan ayah saya sedang bekerja.
Please take off your shoes; it is our custom.	Sila buka kasut anda; inilah adat resam kami.
Have a seat, and I'll bring you a cool drink.	Sila duduk, dan saya akan membawa anda minuman segar.

the official language of Malay, educated Malaysians would speak English as well. A non-Malay Malaysian would also speak his or her own ethnic Chinese or Indian dialect. When speaking Malay there are slight variations between a speaker from Johor in the south and another from Terengganu in the east. The Malay spoken in East Malaysia would also contain slight differences. These minor variations, however, do not generally cause communication problems among Malaysians. Standard Bahasa Malaysia is the language heard on radio and television and taught in schools. Non-Malay language programs shown on Malaysian television channels often have Malay subtitles. The spelling of words in Bahasa Malaysia has been standardized to make the language more or less compatible with Bahasa

Indonesia, a form of Malay spoken by about 100 million Indonesians as their secondary language.

The vocabulary is also being standardized and constantly revised. An educated Indonesian can understand an educated Malaysian, despite a few minor differences between their versions of the Malay language. These differences are not unlike those in the spoken English dialects and vocabularies of Americans, Canadians, and Britons.

Students at class in a private school. Besides the official language, Malay, many Malaysians can speak English as well.

BODY LANGUAGE

Verbal language is not all there is to communication. Body language sometimes does the trick. A shake of the head says "no" in most parts of the world, whereas a nod signifies agreement or acceptance. In Malaysia some gestures are peculiar to an ethnic group, whereas some are common to all. For instance it is generally considered rude to point at people or things with the index finger. A bent index finger or thumb is used to point—or rather to knuckle—in the right direction.

Malaysians do not touch each other unless they are close friends or relatives. In a crowd a woman may hold her dress to herself to avoid touching passersby with it. Muslims greet each other by just touching the other person's right hand and then their own chests. Conservative Muslim women will not shake hands with a man, but will bow gently instead. The old-fashioned Chinese way of greeting—shaking hands at waist level while bowing—is used only by the older Chinese these days.

Similarly the Indian palm-to-palm greeting, *namaskar* (neh-mehs-kehr), is now used only at ceremonial occasions. Among all ethnic groups the Western handshake is increasingly being used as a form of greeting, especially in the business community.

CONTEST OF WORDS

Malaysians respect an articulate, confident speaker. A child's early training in reciting the Koran before an audience is often given as an example of early preparation for public speech.

A traditional form of entertainment at parties is the *pantun* (pahn-toon). Originally a Malay pastime it has become familiar to other Malaysians, especially the Straits Chinese. The men compose humorous quatrains to challenge the women. One of the women answers, usually with the necessary sting. Another man speaks up for his gender, and another woman rebuts. This merry exchange goes on until dawn and is by no means confined to the young. You do not learn to improvise well until you have seen a few birthdays!

A *pantun* can also express tender sentiment, but recited in front of a festive crowd, the message is veiled.

Satellite dishes outside cable network Astro's All Asia Networks Broadcast Center.

THE BROADCAST MEDIA

Broadcasting began in Peninsular Malaysia in 1946 and in East Malaysia in the 1950s. Television was introduced in 1963 and extended to East Malaysia in 1972. Most programs are in Bahasa Malaysia, with airtime also provided for programs in English (mainly from the United States), Chinese and Indian dialects, and East Malaysian regional languages. States have their own radio stations.

Malaysians enjoy many free-to-air television channels, including the state-run Radio Television Malaysia (RTM) TV1 and TV2. There are privately owned channels such as TV3, launched in the mid-1980s; NTV7, launched in

1998; and more recently, TV9 and the main Chinese channel, 8TV. In 2009 Malaysia launched its first music channel, called RTM Muzik Aktif. It is one of the first Malaysian digital channels.

Malaysians also enjoy a wide variety of digital channels on the Astro platform. Astro is the country's main digital satellite channel, broadcasting television and radio programs to 45 percent of Malaysian households. Astro provides Malaysians with access to international documentaries, entertainment shows, news and music, as well as radio content.

In Malaysia there are 19 private and 34 state-owned radio stations. Apart from state-owned radio stations, Malaysians can also enjoy international radio stations such as the BBC World Service, China Radio International, Suara Malaysia, and Voice of Vietnam. Malaysians, particularly the younger generation, are accessing news and entertainment through the Internet. Today there are approximately 16.9 million Internet users and 344,452 Internet hosts (according to a 2010 estimate).

INTERNET LINKS

www.omniglot.com/writing/malay.htm

This is an interesting website that provides a short history of the Malay language, including its writing system in the Arabic and Latin alphabets. It also includes a short guide to Malay pronunciation.

www.mycen.com.my/malaysia/online_news.html

This website provides a comprehensive listing of Malaysia's online press, news portals, independent media, alternative press, Internet news, and news agencies, complete with a search directory.

www.mylanguageexchange.com/learn/malaysia.asp

This website offers the opportunity to learn Bahasa Malaysia online, as well as to practice speaking and writing the language.

Two Chinese opera performers.

10

D

RAMA IN MALAYSIA IS THE product of foreign influence. The best-known dramatic arts in Malaysia are imports: *wayang kulit* (puppet theater) and *bangsawan* (a form of traditional Malay opera) from Indonesia and China.

Making up for the absence of traditional local drama is an impressive body of original Malaysian literature. Some of it was first written in the 19th century, based on oral sources. Some, especially East Malaysian tribal literature, remains unrecorded to this day.

TRADITIONAL LITERATURE

Sagas in which fact and legend blend are known in every state. The stirring tales of Admiral Hang Tuah and his noble fellows are still enjoyed by listeners and readers alike. The history of Malaya has been recorded in *Sejarah Melayu*, the *Malay Annals*. The narrative starts with Alexander the Great, who is described as the ancestor of Malay royalty. As the story gets to the 14th or 15th century, it becomes a verifiable historical record. If

Right: **The puppets used for *wayang kulit* are of intricate design.**

the doings of the 16th-century sultans are not uniformly edifying, they are certainly interesting.

The works of a 19th-century Malay author, Munshi Abdullah, are still studied in schools as literature texts. A much-traveled and well-educated man, Abdullah wrote several books of travels as well as a story of Malay feudal and social history, *Kesah Pelayaran Abdullah* (*Tales from Abdullah's Travels*).

Malaysia also has its own version of Aesop's fables, the most popular being *Hikayat Sang Kanchil*. This is a collection of tales revolving around the adventures of a little mousedeer as it outwits larger and stronger animals and human beings. There is a moral to be learned from each tale, and every Malaysian child knows a story from the entertaining *Hikayat Sang Kanchil*.

DANCE

Traditional dances are popular, but few Malaysians learn them thoroughly. Schoolgirls usually learn the basic movements of a Malay dance called *Bunga Manggar Bunga Raya* or learn dances set to Chinese tunes.

Those who want to dance seriously face hard training, like the Western ballerina. Stress is laid on supple hands—a classical Malay dancer can bend her fingers back to almost touch her forearm!

MAK YONG Mak Yong used to be organized to amuse the sultan's women in the court. *Mak Yong* is a traditional art form incorporating the element of dance, acting, opera, vocal, and instrumental music. It is performed in the Malaysian state of Kelantan.

All the characters in a Mak Yong are played by women, except for the musician. The main dancer, called Mak Yong, produces the story, which is usually about legendary princes and princesses from the oral tradition. They use a few simple hand movements.

The Mak Yong is accompanied by traditional music made up of *gendang*, gongs, *rebab*, and *tetawak*. The main dancer holds a shot bamboo cane that deliberately works to beat the *peran* (clown) on the dance drama.

EAST MALAYSIAN DANCES East Malaysians have preserved many of their people's traditional dances. Dayak children, for example, learn to dance at an early age. The slow but complicated movements of their traditional dances require excellent muscle control. Dancing is supposed to make boys agile and girls graceful.

MALAY DANCE Some old Malay dances have been adapted to modern use. *Ronggeng* and *joget*, traditionally danced by men only before an audience, are performed as "mixed doubles" on the dance floor nowadays. The decencies must be preserved, and of course—throughout the fairly intricate gyrations of a *ronggeng*—the couple never touch each other. Their bodies and arms make reciprocal movements, and their hands almost but never quite meet. A traditional courtly dance is the *Joget Gamelan*. It is danced to the sounds of the xylophone, gong, and drums. The graceful dancers don elaborate costumes complete with a headdress, a silk blouse, and a long silk scarf. To foreign eyes the classical Malay dances have something of a Spanish air, partly because of their common Moorish heritage.

Two dancers performing a traditional Malay dance.

INDIAN DANCE An Indian girl who wants to learn her people's classical dances is advised to start by age 5. There are teachers who are prepared to take a student through her early steps, not forgetting initiation prayers before the Lord Shiva, god of dance, at whose altar she must present her jingling anklets.

Basic classical dancing involves about 100 steps and movements, which are choreographed into dance dramas of old narratives. When the novice reaches her 10th or 11th year, she is ready to perform solo the six major dances of the *Bharatanatyam*, the 16th-century Indian classical dance.

Gongs are an important part of traditional Malay music.

After this display, which is an examination at the same time, the girl will be able to take her place among the mature dancers in temple ceremonies and public performances.

MUSIC OF THE MALAY PENINSULA

The original music of the Malay Peninsula is percussive. Long ago large gongs served to send messages from one place to another. They still give the basic beat for many dances. Whole ensembles of gongs, from huge boomers to delicate tinklers, are used in the Javanese gamelan orchestra, which is occasionally heard in Malaysia, too.

Drums are also played. The man-sized "long drums" of the northern part of the Malay Peninsula are made of hollowed-out tree trunks, the ends of which are covered with taut buffalo or goatskin. Small tambourines are an import from the Arab world. They are beaten to the rhythm of the strident singing of Arab songs at many Malay weddings. The Arabs also brought a type of lute with them, the *gambus*, which is skillfully played by many Malays.

In many villages there is a *keroncong* (kehr-rohng-chohng) band, an ensemble playing old-fashioned music on fiddles, hand-drums, small harmonicas, and sometimes flutes.

Peculiar to the courts of Kedah, Perak, Terengganu, and Selangor is the *nobat* (noh-baht), a band that consists of a straight, valveless silver trumpet, a flute, a gong, and a consort of drums. The *nobat* only performs on ceremonious royal occasions, such as a ruler's accession, wedding, or funeral. The music has a haunting quality. Few who have heard it once can forget the *nobat*.

Malaysia's indigenous peoples, the Orang Asli, have their own brand of tribal music, the sounds of which originate from natural materials such as gourd, cane, wood, and bamboo.

EAST MALAYSIAN MUSIC

In the past, among the people of Sabah and Sarawak, gongs were considered more than musical instruments. Brought into the country by barter trade, they were symbols of wealth and stability as well. Many old rituals involve the use of gongs. The Bidayuh wash their ancestral head trophies in an overturned gong filled with coconut water. Iban bridal couples sit on a pair of gongs.

A man playing a mouth organ.

Many reed and bamboo flutes are used in East Malaysia. Some, those that resemble the Jew's harp, produce a sound so soft it can only be heard by someone near the performer. Others are used at ceremonies and parties and can be quite shrill. Flute tunes are usually brief motifs of arpeggios, repeated over and over again with minor variations. It is not common for people to sing when wind instruments arc being played. Natives of Borneo also play a mouth organ that has bamboo pipes that stand up and a gourd that serves as a wind chamber.

A string instrument native to Sabah is the *jotong utong* (bamboo zither). A thick piece of bamboo has strips of its skin lifted up; each section is pegged with little wedges to stretch and tune it. The wood xylophone consists of hardwood sticks of varying lengths stretched on a string ladder.

MODERN MUSIC

Much Malaysian patriotic music would sound sentimental to the foreign ear. Love for the nation is expressed in the same swooning tones and words that are used in love songs, often in tunes strongly reminiscent of Indonesian *keroncong*.

On big occasions and at rallies, processions, and open-air functions, sentiment gives way to big drums and brass bands. They can rival the

A school marching band performs during a parade celebrating Malaysia's independence.

best when it comes to oom-pah-pah. Military units, the police, schools, and even private firms maintain brass bands of varying quality.

In the 1960s Malaysians, just like many music lovers all over the world, were greatly influenced by the music of the Beatles, Elvis Presley, and other rock-and-roll bands from the West. In the 1979s and 1980s homegrown artists such as Sudirman, Sharifah Aini, and Sheila Majid dominated the local music scene. Rock and heavy metal music became very popular and local rock bands such as Search and Wings were well known among Malaysian fans.

Today the young enjoy all types of music from the international music scene, especially rap, hip-hop, and pop music, just like their Western counterparts. In addition to Western artists Malay teens may also listen to bands from neighboring Indonesia. Teenagers from the Chinese ethnic group may follow Chinese bands from Taiwan, Hong Kong, and even Japan. Teenagers from the Indian ethnic groups may listen to music from parts of India and Sri Lanka. Among the Sikhs, Punjabi music or *bhangra* is popular. Since the 1990s certain musicians have started to create music that is influenced by Islam. These bands have a large following in more rural areas.

One of the most successful singers in Malaysia today is Siti Nurhaliza, whose works include Malay pop and Malay traditional music. In 2005 MTV Asia ranked her as the second-biggest Asian artist at the MTV Asia Awards in Bangkok, and in 2008 she was named one of Asia's Idols by Asia News Network.

VISUAL ART

Malaysia shares with Indonesia the tradition of batik—wax-resistant fabric printing used in cloth production. In recent years, however, batik has also become an accepted artistic medium.

Young painters have branched off from the traditional, Dutch-inspired style used by old masters such as Mohammad Hoessein bin Enas, a well-known portrait painter who uses mainly oils. Young painters experiment with abstract renditions of their ideas in modern media such as tempera, acrylic, and collage.

Chinese brush painting is an art form brought to Malaysia by Chinese immigrants that is now well established. Besides traditional motifs some painters depict local scenery, fruit, insects, and wildlife in the quick, fluid brush strokes typical of this style.

Contemporary Malaysian artists are beginning to gain international recognition and this is being reflected in the sale price of their art works. In 2008 a computer-manipulated art work called *Huminodun* by Malaysian artist Yee I-Lann was sold for RM117,000 (approximately US$37,117) at a Christie's auction in Hong Kong. In the same year the work of three other Malaysian artists fetched record-high prices—Ahmad Zakii Anwar's representation of a Buddha sold for an impressive 213,000 ringgit (approximately US$67,682), a piece by popular artist Jai sold for 196,000 ringgit (approximately US$62,280), and veteran artist Chang Fee Ming's watercolor collage sold for 130,000 ringgit (approximately US$41,308) at an art fair in China's capital, Beijing.

Malaysia has plans to establish itself as a regional hub for contemporary art. High-quality pieces of art can be found in Kuala Lumpur's Galeri Petronas. The gallery, established in Kuala Lumpur in 1993, showcases works of art by Malaysian as well as foreign artists. It runs exhibitions and programs to promote art to all Malaysians.

PUBLIC SPEAKING AS AN ART

Malaysians of all races value an articulate speaker who can stand up and say his piece on any occasion. There is a body of traditional literature that was only preserved orally until the quite recent past. Some of it is still unrecorded and in danger of being lost.

The traditional pastimes survive to a limited extent in the kampung and longhouses of remote areas. They are also enjoying a new lease on life as public entertainment. At official and private functions it is it is possible to hear a recitation of an excerpt of one of the interminable *syair* (shah-eer) stories or a Mak Yong performance.

Schools organize rhetoric and speech contests to encourage students to speak confidently and freely. Debating societies are popular among schoolchildren, particularly in Chinese schools, and interschool debates are "fought" by proper rules in general, with regional variants.

HANDICRAFTS

One of Malaysia's most distinctive handicrafts, organized as a small industry in many rural places, is batik. Batik material has all kinds of uses in Malaysia, including clothing, tablecloths, and curtains. Good quality batik shirts are considered appropriate dress for men on formal occasions and at celebrations, be they weddings, business meetings, or diplomatic functions.

Batik is produced mainly on the eastern coast of the peninsula, from where it is sold to other parts of Malaysia and to Indonesia, Thailand, and

Locals use batik cloth for a wide range of purposes and tourists are attracted to its unique patterns and vibrant colors.

Singapore. Sarawak's Iban people produce a labor-intensive cloth called *ikat* (ee-kaht). Before weaving, the threads are dipped in dyes extracted from forest plants—usually black, red, or yellow ochre. The threads are dyed so that abstract geometric shapes or stylized forms of crocodiles, lizards, and snakes only appear when the fabric is woven.

In Sarawak Borneo's best backstrap loom weavers can still be found. Iban women tie-dye the warp threads of their cotton fabric into intricate traditional patterns. When the cloth is woven, the ready-made patterns appear. In the past Malaysian men were expert woodcarvers who liked to beautify articles of daily use with fretwork, whittling, or surface incision. The fascia boards of old-fashioned Malay houses are often thus decorated, as are women's weaving utensils, game boards, headboards, and mirror frames.

INTERNET LINKS

www.galeripetronas.com.my

This website provides an avenue for artists, both Malaysian and foreign, to display their works in order to meet and nourish the growing interest of the Malaysian public in visual arts.

www.dancemalaysia.com

This website provides an introduction to the dances, the artists, dance companies, institutions, and various performances. It is a valuable resource center for students who wish to begin research, producers trying to locate talent, and anyone who is interested in dance.

www.acgmalaysia.com

This website is a platform dedicated to Malaysia's arts and craft guild, promoting awareness of the arts and crafts among the public and acting as a resource center, providing information about art supplies, workshops, galleries, and art and craft techniques.

LEISURE

A boy flying a kite in a rural village in Sabah. Kite-flying competitions among villages are common in Malaysia.

11

MANY OF MALAYSIA'S POPULAR pastimes involve some form of competition. Malaysians spend a lot of free time with family and friends.

CHILDHOOD GAMES

Malaysian children enjoy games such as hopscotch, jacks, and "rock, paper, scissors," called *kuncum* (koon-choom). On the count of *kuncum*, each player makes a hand symbol: two pointed fingers for scissors, an open palm for paper, or a clenched fist for rock. Who wins depends on the combination of symbols. The scissors cut the paper, the rock breaks the scissors, and the paper wraps the rock.

Kite flying is another popular activity that are enjoyed by both children and adults alike. There are even kite flying competitions. The kite line is dipped in glue and then in powdered glass, so it will cut an opponent's line if skillfully flown. Kite-flying competitions are held among villages. The champions are grown men.

Spinning tops can be used for fighting, as can *quoits*, which are somewhat like pitching horseshoes. An elaborate version of coconut shy involves throwing half a coconut shell over prizes. If the shell covers an item, the contestant can claim it.

In the past schoolchildren had fighting fish in jars and fighting beetles in matchboxes. Their elder brothers used to play a more exciting game—cockfighting—that strikes most foreigners as cruel, even though it is illegal in Malaysia.

FISHING

Malaysians have an abiding love for fish and fishing. Almost every settlement is near a river or the sea. The boat jetty or harbor wall is sure to be populated with men and boys using a variety of tackle. Urban wage earners make weekend trips to promising spots such as waterfalls, rapids, a quiet bridge, or an old embankment that promises undisturbed communion with the fish.

Many people like to stretch nets across little rivers or set traps. A common fish trap looks like a long round basket, with an entry hole defended by tapering rattan rods. A fish can get in but not out. The owner of the trap opens a little hinged door in the side of the basket to collect his catch.

Malaysians' well-known love for water and fishing has led to a small industry that provides accommodation in modest seaside and riverside huts or elegantly styled "chalets" that are rented out by the day or week. Such shelters are usually very basic, with a sleeping room, a cooking facility, and some sort of washroom. The rent is paid for the whole unit; the owner does not care how many people are jammed into it for a few days. Families, school classes, clubs—any group that cannot afford to stay at a proper "beach resort"—get all the fun of beach, river, or island entertainment at a modest price.

WATER SPORTS AND BEACH LIFE

There are many beach resorts in Malaysia, and very elegant ones at that. Hotels and clubs on the wide beaches of the eastern coast of Peninsular Malaysia and Borneo invite the affluent vacationer to a sunny stay filled with windsurfing, snorkeling, scuba diving, sailing, or simply lounging on the warm sand. Malaysian beach resorts are popular with tourists and locals alike.

Malaysia has the natural advantage of a tropical climate. Occasionally it can be too windy or too rainy for outdoor sports, but it is never too cold. Even during the rainy season some fine days can be enjoyed by water sports enthusiasts and beach lovers.

Malaysia's larger towns have their own water sports clubs and facilities. Scuba diving is a new sport that is catching on fast among affluent Malaysians. Even in some kampungs boys may be seen equipped with snorkels, flippers, and diving goggles and chasing the sea and river fish with their bamboo fishing spears.

A diver observes a green turtle in the waters of Sipadan, one of Malaysia's most popular dive sites.

LAND SPORTS

BALL GAMES Soccer and cricket caught on like wildfire in the Malaysia in the early 20th century. Soccer continues to be very popular today, along with basketball, table tennis, golf, and badminton.

There is also a local sport, somewhat resembling volleyball, called *sepak takraw* (say-pahk tahk-raw). It means "hit the ball." *Sepak takraw* is one of Malaysia's most exciting sports. Originating in the courts of Siam (Thailand) and Melaka, the game used to involve two or more players who formed a circle and kicked, shouldered, and headed a hollow rattan ball to one another. The object was to keep the ball from touching the ground. Players may use their heels, soles, insteps, thighs, shoulders, and heads—in fact everything but their hands.

Kampong boys still play the game this way. Exact rules were drawn up in 1946, and a net, as well as a proper scoring system, was introduced. The game was formally included in the Southeast Asia Games in 1965, played by teams from Malaysia, Brunei, Indonesia, Thailand, Burma, Singapore, and the Philippines.

MARTIAL ARTS *Silat* is an old Malay form of self-defense, not unlike shadowboxing. Small boys are taught the basic movements, unarmed. Mock fighting is not encouraged by *silat* masters until the combatants have learned discipline and restraint.

In urban areas other forms of self-defense are popular. Many join taekwondo classes, kicking their feet over their heads with great gusto.

Older people are sometimes seen in the town parks, in the cool of dawn, practicing slow, rhythmic movements called Tai Chi. This very ancient Chinese martial art, now much prized as a form of exercise, is believed to strengthen the body without exhausting or overstraining it.

Malaysia's Noor Parahara (*right*) makes a strike at her opponent, Laos' Boutsady Souavong, during the 2009 Pencak Silat event at the Southeast Asian Games.

MUSIC

Malaysians of all ages enjoy making music and singing together. Many Malaysians are members of church or secular choirs, and many children belong to school choirs.

Chinese music enthusiasts get together to form chamber groups. These dispense with the percussion that gives Chinese opera its deafening resonance, using knee-fiddles, flutes, lutes, and sometimes one softly played tambourine.

In the towns formal Western music lessons are available, and many middle-class children are encouraged to learn to play the piano or violin. Malaysian music students take British examinations from the Royal School of Music or Trinity College.

DRAMATIC PURSUITS

Traditional Malay opera is called *bangsawan*. Once a traveling show it is believed to have originated from India. The stories and characters are developed from diverse sources, including Indian, Chinese, Indonesian, and Malay.

Wayang performers preparing for their performance.

The involved plot was broken by unconnected interludes called "extra turns" that permitted one actor to garner a little separate applause and maybe a shower of coins. Stories and music were often improvised by the performers.

Many *bangsawan* performers were children, who were bought from their parents or shadier sources for this trade. The court books of the prewar period are full of complaints against *bangsawan* masters ill-using their charges or even kidnapping pretty children before the show moved on to another town. *Bangsawan* is very much a dying art form, and today it is difficult to find any *bangsawan* performers in Malaysia.

The famous Indonesian shadow play, *wayang kulit*, has been adopted by Malaysian performers. Puppets cut out of stiff leather are manipulated with a set of movable sticks behind a white sheet illuminated by a couple of kerosene lanterns.

Chinese opera—called *wayang* (wah-young)—is a form of drama with close religious connections. A temple deity's birthday is often celebrated with an opera. The hungry ghosts that are believed to roam the land during the Chinese seventh month are generally appeased with lavish operatic performances. Quite young actors may get their early training in silent parts, as attendants or messengers, before graduating to play the parts of a prince, emperor, general, princess, or queen. Although the roles of the emperor or the general are always sung by men, the part of the prince, especially in a romantic work, may be performed by a young woman. The part requires a very high tenor voice, and the character is supposed to look "sweet."

Spectators at the Asian X-Games and Junior X-Games qualifiers.

One ancient Malaysian spectator art is storytelling. Especially in the days when hardly anyone could read, before radio and television provided evening entertainment, a practiced storyteller could be sure of an enthralled audience. There is a Malay method of chanting a historical tale, called *syair*, which regularly entertained choice gatherings at royal parties.

One Sarawak story takes nine nights to tell. Longhouse festivals may involve three or four reciters who walk up and down the long veranda for up to eight hours without once stopping before their story-song is done.

HAVING FUN

Malaysians love spending their leisure time eating and catching up with friends and family either at home or in a restaurant, café, or street food stall. Many social activities start with a meal followed by a trip to a shopping mall or cinema to enjoy a movie. Malaysians like to be in a crowd—grannies, babies, and the entire family often come out together to eat, shop, and watch the latest movies.

Live sporting events, especially soccer, never fail to attract huge crowds. To secure good seats spectators arrive several hours before the match is scheduled to begin. Fans can be sure that hundreds of little food and drink stands will surround the stadium, enabling them to have a picnic while watching the players. Malaysians follow sports mainly on television, and often place bets on the outcome.

After school many youngsters will wander around shopping malls with their group of friends. They will meet friends, share ice cream and drinks, and window shop. Among the young movie theaters are popular entertainment spots, as are skating rinks and bowling alleys.

GOLD RUSH SYNDROME

Malaysians love to be wherever something is happening. An innocent notice in a newspaper or a rumor spread by word of mouth can spark off a mass movement. Lines may snake toward a spring that is said to have incredible healing powers. A miracle healer may attract a sudden influx of patients to a roadless village. A report on the sighting of a supernatural phenomenon in a lake or river or on a beach will draw crowds of sightseers. In any case everyone has a good time whether or not the object of curiosity shows up.

Occasionally an actual small gold rush breaks out in Malaysia. A farmer finds gold dust or what he considers to be raw diamonds in his field. Within days the place will be swarming with prospectors, each armed with a large flat pan called a *dulang* (doo-lahng), used for washing soil to extract the precious mineral. The gold may prove scanty or entirely absent, and the village will return to normal in good time.

INTERNET LINKS

www.steveninteractive.com/marfima

This website is a comprehensive portal of the Malaysian Leisure and Recreation Council (MARFIMA). It was established in the 1988 under the guidance of the Ministry of Youth and Sports Malaysia to promote and develop leisure and recreation activities among the community.

enwww.nsc.gov.my

This is the official website of the Malaysian Sports Council, an organization formed to promote excellence in sports.

malaysia.tourism-asia.net/malaysia-holidays.html

This website is a guide to various leisure activities in Malaysia, including golf, diving, whitewater rafting, river safari, cave exploring, bird watching, and much more.

FESTIVALS

Bajau horsemen at the annual festival of horsemanship in Kota Belud.

12

I N THE COURSE OF A YEAR MALAYSIANS enjoy numerous public holidays to celebrate the religions and major festivals of the three main races—the Malays, Chinese, and Indians. Even if a Malaysian does not belong to the religion or culture that celebrates a particular festival, he or she will visit friends who do.

CHINESE NEW YEAR

Celebrating the new year is a bit of a problem in Malaysia. Which new year do you mean? There is the "ordinary" or "Western" New Year on January 1, the Chinese New Year, the Muslim New Year, and the Hindu New Year. Each is celebrated by some Malaysians, although the Chinese New Year must take the prize for noise and hilarity.

The Chinese New Year marks the beginning of a new lunar year; thus it falls on a different date each year. It can be as early as December or as late as March, but it usually falls in January or February. Chinese New Year lasts for 15 days.

During the New Year stores shut down for several days and businesses

Right: A lion dance performance during Chinese New Year.

113

ANNUAL FESTIVALS

January/February	Chinese New Year
	Chap Goh Mei (Chinese)
	Thaiponggal (Hindu)
	Thaipusam (Hindu)
March/April	Good Friday (Christian)
May	Wesak Day (Buddhist)
May 30—31	Kadazan Harvest Festival (Kadazan)
June 1—2	Gawai Dayak (Sarawak natives)
August 31	National Day
October/November	Deepavali (Hindu)
December 25	Christmas (Christian)

The dates of the Islamic festivals—Hari Raya Puasa, Hari Raya Haji, Ma'al Hijrah, and the Prophet Muhammad's birthday—follow the Islamic lunar calendar and can fall in a different month from one year to the next.

The dates of the Hindu and Buddhist festivals follow the Indian and Chinese lunar calendars and change from year to year, though not as drastically as the Islamic festival dates.

come to a standstill, while bosses and workers hold family reunions, enjoy huge feasts, gamble a little "for luck" (unless they lose), and visit relatives and friends.

At midnight some parts of the large towns burst into a cacophony of firecrackers. Firecrackers are officially banned in Malaysia, but some traditional Chinese families ignore the ban, because firecrackers are supposed to drive out evil spirits. They are also great entertainment. On New Year's Day, when visitors come to each open house, the boys are likely to fire off a volley of firecrackers each time a particularly respected guest makes his way up the garden path. Chinese New Year is also celebrated by lion and dragon dances. The lion dance is believed to bring good luck and fortune. So, during the Chinese New Year, troupes of lion dancers are invited to Chinese homes and businesses to perform the traditional custom of *cai ching*, which literally means "plucking the greens." The "lion's" task is to successfully pluck the auspicious green vegetables. If successful the lion and troupe will be rewarded with a red envelope that contains money.

CHAP GOH MEI

Celebrated on the 15th day after the Chinese New Year, on the night of a full moon, Chap Goh Mei fulfills the function that Twelfth Night does after Christmas: It marks the official end of the festivities.

Modern-day Chap Goh Mei is usually celebrated with a big family dinner. Many Chinese hang out red lanterns or switch on electric "fairy lights," and children let off the remnants of the firecrackers bought for the Chinese New Year.

In the past a troupe of mediums gave displays of firewalking at temples. Under the protection of a deity the participants ran or walked barefoot on burning coals in a pit 10 feet (3 m) long. Some mediums may lie down on the bed of coals unscorched and let the others walk over them.

THAIPONGGAL

Thaiponggal is a harvest festival, celebrated unseasonably in January, because it is fixed on the Hindu calendar. Farmers rise while it is still dark and cook some of the newly harvested grain to present it to the sun at dawn. This is the *ponggal*.

Some urban families have adapted this ritual to their living conditions. The family rises, bathes, and gets dressed before dawn, without using any light. When all are ready in their best clothes, they assemble around a display of fruit and flowers. Lamps are lit. The first sight in the morning must be a vision of natural beauty. Dawn arrives, and a vegetarian breakfast is enjoyed by all.

THAIPUSAM

This festival is celebrated in the streets, with all the noise and excitement of a carnival. The day is consecrated to the Hindu deity Lord Subramaniam to celebrate his victory over evil forces and to fulfill vows made to him during the year.

Hindu devotees march in the streets in a long procession, carrying colorful displays of flowers and fruit. Libations of milk and honey are made in honor of the deity.

A Hindu devotee carrying an elaborate *kavadi* during the Thaipusam procession in Kuala Lumpur.

A Hindu redeeming vows carries a *kavadi* (kah-vah-dee). This is a fancifully decorated structure that is balanced on skewers inserted into the bearer's back and arms or attached to the flesh by steel hooks and chains. To increase the penance, additional skewers may be stuck through the penitent's cheeks or tongue.

The amazing part of a *kavadi* procession is not how seemingly easily the entranced penitents carry their burdens, but the fact that half an hour after the event, when the skewers have been removed, the penitents appear to have sustained neither wounds nor swellings on their bodies.

The most famous procession is held at Kuala Lumpur's Batu Caves, where 800,000 spectators gather to watch penitents climb the steep flight of 272 steps up to a shrine housed in a limestone cave.

KADAZAN HARVEST FESTIVAL

This harvest festival is celebrated in the East Malaysian state of Sabah. Although it has been named after Sabah's major indigenous tribe, the Kadazan, all Sabah natives keep the solemnity and everyone else joins in the festivities.

This holiday is based on the Kadazan's worship of ancient gods, including the rice spirit Bambaazon, who is revered in rice plants, rice grains, and cooked rice. Without rice there is no life. Kadazan children are taught from an early age never to spill or waste any of the precious grain and to pay special respect to the gods whenever the village reaps a good rice harvest.

The harvest festival is a time when many Sabah natives take their traditional clothes out of the closet and put them on for a few days. The event is celebrated with public gatherings and family parties and an open house to all visitors. *Air tapai* (ah-yay tah-pie), a homemade rice wine, is freely given to all.

Gawai Dayak celebrations.

GAWAI DAYAK

Tracing its roots back to as early as 1957, the Gawai Dayak or Dayak festival has only been celebrated as a public holiday since 1964. It is celebrated every year on June 1. Previously Sarawak's indigenous tribes held their own harvest festivals at their own times, but with the establishment of the festival, the celebrations have been put on an official footing.

Gawai is held in towns as well as in longhouses, with traditional costume parades and competitions. For some people this is the only time of the year when they wear their beautiful but somewhat cumbersome traditional outfits. The Gawai showcases the Iban women's silver jewelry and the Orang Ulus' priceless antique beads.

Gawai Dayak is celebrated with an open house, official parties and receptions, and streams of *tuak* (too-ahk), a homemade rice wine. In longhouses offerings of food are made to the gods of rice and prosperity and blessed by waving a chicken over the display.

Muslims gathering for prayers at the National Mosque during the Muslim New Year.

MUSLIM FESTIVALS

HARI RAYA PUASA This marks the end of the fasting month of Ramadan, when for 30 days Muslims take no food or drink from dawn to dusk.

Before Hari Raya Puasa, houses are cleaned and given a new coat of paint. New curtains are made, new clothes sewn, and huge quantities of special foods are prepared.

On Hari Raya morning the men and boys in the family go to the mosque for prayers, after which the family visits the graves of their departed loved ones. The rest of the day is spent visiting the homes of friends and relatives where a colorful array of food is served.

HARI RAYA HAJI This festival commemorates Ibrahim's (Abraham's) willingness to sacrifice his son Ismail (Ishmael) at Allah's (God's) bidding. It is celebrated in particular by Muslims who have made the hajj, the required pilgrimage to Mecca. The men attend the Hari Raya Haji prayers at the mosque, after which some of the worshipers perform animal sacrifices. For Muslims making the hajj, prayers offered on this day mark the end of the pilgrimage.

MA'AL HIJRAH (AWAL MUHARRAM) Ma'al Hijrah is the first day on the Islamic calendar—that is, it marks the start of the new year for Muslims. More important it is the anniversary of the Prophet Muhammad's flight from Mecca to Medina. Ma'al Hijrah commemorates the beginning of Islam as a separate religion.

According to the Islamic or Hijri calendar, the current year is 1432 A.H. (Anno Hegirae), which began approximately December 7, 2010 and will last until November 6, 2011.

THE PROPHET MUHAMMAD'S BIRTHDAY   The birthday of the founder of Islam, the Prophet Muhammad, is commemorated by Muslims. It falls on the 12th day of the month of Rabi-ul-Awal, which was February 15 in 2011. As a public holiday the Prophet Muhammad's birthday is celebrated with special prayers, processions, and religious rallies.

OTHER FESTIVALS

Other major festivals celebrated in Malaysia include Wesak Day, a celebration of the Buddha's birth, death, and enlightenment, when Buddhists make visits to the temples to offer prayers; Chinese All Souls' Day, a day set aside by the Chinese to visit and clean ancestral graves and offer food to the spirits of their ancestors; Deepavali, an important Hindu festival celebrated by Hindu Indians; and Christmas, although it is not celebrated in as big a way as in the United States—in Malaysia, it is more a time of super sales at department stores.

INTERNET LINKS

www.allmalaysia.info/msiaknow/festivals.htm

This is a guide to all major festivals and celebrations in Malaysia, such as Hari Raya Puasa, Chinese New Year, Deepavali, and Christmas.

www.go2travelmalaysia.com/tour_malaysia/holidays.htm

This website is a comprehensive portal that provides a handy listing of all the national public holidays in Malaysia. This Internet link includes a list of specific holidays only celebrated by certain states.

www.cultureshocktherapy.com/region-my-94.php

This website is instrumental in providing an interesting account of the unique Thaipusam festival celebrated in Malaysia, complete with colorful photographs.

FOOD

A street stall selling sweets and cakes.

13

> **HAVE YOU EATEN YOUR RICE?"** is a common greeting in Malaysia. Most Malaysians eat rice at least once a day. Rice is central to a Malaysian meal. Malaysians serve food and dine in many ways. They may use a pair of chopsticks and eat out of a bowl, spread their food out on a banana leaf and eat with their fingers, or eat with a fork and a spoon from a plate.

Fresh food is available all year-round. Careful housewives buy fresh greens and small amounts of fresh meat or fish from the wet market on a daily basis. Grocery shopping at a modern supermarket has become more popular, but the wet market, with its fresh produce and negotiable prices, is still by far the best place to shop for everyday food items.

Fish is a universal favorite in Malaysia. People of all ages and religions eat fish. Seafood, including prawns and crab, are equally popular. Meat is usually cooked in soups or the ubiquitous curry and cut into bite-sized pieces before serving. Malaysians also enjoy Western-style food such as steak and fast foods, but most prefer their own cuisine.

WHAT'S COOKING?

In towns bottled gas or electricity is used for cooking. In Miri, Sarawak, gas is piped throughout the town and sold to consumers at a cheap rate. Microwave ovens, electric rice cookers, and toasters—all the labor-saving kitchen devices of modern times—have made their appearance in Malaysian kitchens.

In the countryside many housewives have gas stoves too, although some still use kerosene burners. The traditional village hearth is a clay slab placed on the kitchen floor or on a ledge. Here a fire is kindled in the morning and the cooking pots placed over it on iron tripods or stones. Fish or whatever is to be cooked is laid across green branches to grill or suspended at a height to smoke.

The old-fashioned Chinese housewife uses a charcoal stove, a round pot with a small grate in which a charcoal fire is fanned to life. Not many households today rely entirely on this fuel. However, should a power outage occur, the housewife may be glad to have a charcoal pot substitute sitting in the corner of the kitchen.

Strict Hindus who belong to the high castes have complicated and demanding dietary laws, one of which demands that all their food be cooked in pure brass pots. The modern alternative is stainless steel. Some families keep one set of utensils for the orthodox members and a separate one for the more liberal.

TABLE MANNERS

Table manners are not strictly restricted to the table. Many Malaysians eat on clean mats spread on the floor, and they are quite as conscious of decorum as anybody else is.

An essential rule, especially among Muslims, is that only the right hand may be used for eating. It is washed in fresh water before the meal. The left hand is considered unclean because it is used to clean oneself after a visit to the restroom. The right hand is used to scoop up rice, pick tidbits from the various cooked dishes, or roll up a morsel of *sambal belacan* (sahm-bahl beh-lah-chahn)—a condiment of prawn paste, ground chili peppers, and lime juice—in a blanched leaf. The little finger is not used for holding food; the others are used only up to the second knuckle. Soup is served in individual bowls and eaten with a spoon.

After the meal in a Malay household, a dish of water is passed around; small children may have to wash their whole hand, but anybody with good manners only needs to rinse the thumb and three fingers.

Casual visitors are asked to partake of any meal the family may be having. If they are formally invited guests, they may be served separately from the family.

In conservative households the women and children eat by themselves after the men have had their fill. It is a matter of some importance for a boy to be promoted to eat with his father once he reaches a certain age. This may be after he has passed important school examinations or some other such rite of passage.

The "eating order" may even be extended—men eat first, women and little children who need help with eating next, and servants eat last.

FOOD TABOOS

The most obvious food taboo in an officially Muslim nation is the prohibition on pork. Pork-free food is certified *halal* (hah-lahl) to indicate to Muslim customers that it is not forbidden.

Hindus and Sikhs do not eat beef, although they use milk products in their diets. Some Hindus also avoid eggs; others consume only food that does not involve killing. Buddhists avoid dairy products, such as egg, butter, and cheese. They get protein from soybeans and other vegetable products such as lentils.

Such restrictions can be problematic when cooking for a special function such as a party. It is normal to ask guests if they eat pork or beef to sort out what may be served to each guest.

An unexpected visitor at mealtime must be offered food. He may try to decline, but a proper Malaysian host will insist until the visitor has agreed to eat something.

Home-cooked food is eaten without comment. Sniffing food is regarded as very rude by most Malaysians. Refusing food by touching the dish with the right hand is acceptable.

DRINKING

Muslims do not drink alcohol. However, beer can be purchased in most urbanized areas of Malaysia and is drunk by the Chinese and Indians. In certain rural areas of Malaysia, such as the eastern coast of the peninsula, it is quite common to find signs stating, "Muslims will not be served alcohol" in coffee shops and restaurants.

Some Indian Malaysians like to brew their own alcohol. A kind of wine called toddy can be made from sugarcane juice and the sap of several palms, such as the coconut and the *nipah* (nee-pah). The bud stems of the palm are slightly cut and the juice oozing out is collected in small vessels, then emptied into a jar and fermented with or without the addition of yeast. Good toddy is refreshing and slightly lighter than beer.

Borneo natives make a sort of beer out of cooked glutinous rice and homemade yeast. It tastes not unlike Japanese sake, although the quality is seldom standard. The drink is called *tuak* or *air tapai*.

Locally produced *tuak*, or rice wine.

Rice beer and toddy can be distilled into high-grade alcohol called *arrak*. Unskilled processing or the addition of other substances can make this homemade beverage dangerous. Cases of death and serious illness from drinking *arrak* have occasionally been reported.

Malaysians like company when they drink. Some communities have "drinking songs." Among these the chants of Sarawak's Kayans hold a special place. They originated when a high-ranking chief of old refused to drink unless the woman offering him the glass sang a song and everyone else present repeated the chorus.

AN *ULAM* SPREAD

Visitors to Malaysia might occasionally see adults or children picking an oily looking creeper leaf from a hedge or an inconspicuous fern shoot from the undergrowth by the side of the road. "To *ulam* (ooh-lahm) with our lunch!" they explain to a curious passerby.

Ulam is a popular dish among Malaysians, regardless of ethnicity. An *ulam* spread consists largely of prawn, fish, and a variety of vegetables, including leaves, creepers, beans, cucumber, and cabbage. Malaysian children who live in the countryside know how to pick out the edible shoots from the inedible ones. To top it all off, a spicy sauce called *sambal* adds spike to the spread. *Nasi ulam* is made by frying rice with shredded vegetables, sliced chilies, fish flakes, and small prawns.

Sometimes *ulam* vegetables are blanched in boiling water for a minute or so. In a dysentery-prone area where raw food often carries germs, this is a wise precaution.

The absence of meat makes *ulam* especially appropriate for the Muslim menu, as Muslims are not allowed to eat pork or meat that has not been slaughtered in the name of Allah.

WEDDING FEASTS

In most cultures weddings are occasions to have a feast. However solemn the ceremony may be, once the priests and elders have performed the rites, everyone adjourns to a sumptuous feast. In rural areas the whole village participates in a wedding, but urban couples send their wedding invitations only to as many family members and friends as the budget will allow. Some Malaysian parents, however, are willing to incur heavy debts just to give their son or daughter a grand wedding party.

An important part of Malay wedding plans concerns money matters: Who will pay for what and how much can be spent? In rural areas the groom's contribution is brought to the bride's house in a merry procession of unmarried girls who carry decorated foodstuffs and banknotes pleated into flowers. As a token of their mutual caring and sharing, the bride and groom are made to "feed" one another after the wedding ceremony.

Chinese couples announce their engagement by distributing a special kind of sweet among their families and friends. It is made of finely ground peanuts and spun sugar, often packed together with slabs of peanut toffee. Love is sweet! The wedding dinner itself may consist of 10 or 12 courses, each one finer (and more expensive) than the one before.

The feast for a Sikh wedding is prepared by the community's elders in the temple. The main work of catering is the responsibility of a team of stalwart men, who are experts in the production of unleavened bread and huge tubs of curry.

PICNIC FOOD

In some cultures a picnic means sandwiches and an easy day for the cook; Malaysians take picnics much more seriously.

Food usually includes rice, regardless of where you are in Malaysia. Whether the picnickers are a busload of students or Boy Scouts on a field trip or a sports or fishing group having a gathering, they are sure to make provisions for cooking and eating rice. On arriving at the picnic spot, the party may build a little fire. The more responsible members of the group then begin boiling the rice and pounding the spices for the *sambal*. Then the food is served on large leaves plucked from a tree and wiped clean. Eating is done with the fingers.

Nasi lemak with vegetables and curried meat, also known as *rendang*.

Some Malaysian picnickers bring cold cooked rice packed with a spicy condiment in a large banana leaf. Called *nasi lemak* (nah-si leh-mah), this used to be the classic fare to take on school picnics, and the preparation of so many picnic packs at a go required a lot of patience and had to begin long before dawn.

A Malaysian seaside picnic may take the whole weekend. The members of the group bring along fishing tackle, hooks and lines, nets, and crab traps. Their freshly caught seafood and fish are flipped from the line or net on to a rough little grill constructed out of green sticks to be roasted to perfection. An upcountry picnic party does not rely on its guns for provisions. To supplement or substitute for a fresh catch, canned foods are carried along, in particular *ikan sardin* (ee-kahn sahr-din)—canned mackerel or tuna.

FOOD CAN BE GOOD FOR THE SOUL

Special sweets tell the world that a Chinese couple is engaged. A triangular rice dumpling is given to friends on the day of the Dragon Boat Festival. Romantic stories are told about the plump, rich moon cakes exchanged during the Moon Cake or Lantern Festival.

The Bidayuh of Sarawak have a new year's ceremony during which a member from each household sets out with a basket full of rice cakes and presents each family in the village with one piece. While the messenger is out an emissary from every family in the village similarly visits his or her house, returning the same present many times over.

At the Gawai a harvest festival celebrated by Borneo natives, visitors are not only royally feasted but are also pressed to take basketfuls of special cakes home with them. Let nobody say the hosts are stingy!

A Malay rice cake, the *ketupat* (keh-too-paht), is steamed in a square case of coconut leaf. For festive occasions the cases can be fashioned into fish or bird shapes, designs limited only by the skill of the manufacturer. During holiday seasons there are *ketupat*-making contests in some villages, emphasizing either speed or beauty.

Indian foods for festival consumption are beautifully colored and sometimes decorated with paper-thin pieces of gold or silver. On the occasion of Deepavali, the festival of lights, the dividing line between food and art is blurred: One of the most beautiful decorations consists of large, intricate designs drawn on the floor with colored rice.

EATING OUT IN MALAYSIA

With a climate that favors outdoor activity and a gregarious nature, Malaysians enjoy eating out all year-round at a range of food centers and restaurants with Malay, Chinese, Indian, and international fare.

The bigger towns have hawker centers where dozens of individual cooks set up little kitchens to prepare rice, noodles, fish and meat dishes, vegetarian selections, sweet and spicy dishes—any dish imaginable—while you wait

A street food vendor. Street food in Malaysia is both delicious and affordable and available late into the night.

at one of the tables. Traveling hawkers offer most urban neighborhoods steamed dumplings, a variety of noodle dishes cooked on portable stoves, grilled meat, ice cream, and cold drinks.

A small town, a ferry point, or a river jetty is sure to have at least a couple of noodle stalls and a drink vendor, maybe a "coconut man" who lops the top off the green globe and extracts the fruit's sweet water for sale.

Malaysians even like going out for breakfast. In the cool of the morning they congregate around small tables under trees or big umbrella shades outside coffee shops. Rice gruel spooned boiling hot over a raw egg is a favorite. Salted and fried tidbits are eaten with this as a relish to add flavor. Noodles of different shapes and colors—long, flat, fat, stringy, white, yellow—are prepared to customers' tastes and served with soup or dry, bland or fiercely spiced. Breakfast "bread" is available in the form of Indian pancakes eaten with meat or lentil curry sauces. Malaysians with conservative tastes enjoy *nasi lemak* for breakfast, too.

Halal restaurants serving international cuisines—Italian, Japanese, Mexican, Vietnamese, Mediterranean, North Indian, Thai—may be the choice for less casual outings.

FAST FOOD

Fast food is extremely popular among the younger generation in Malaysia. In many towns there is now a hamburger joint, although the product is called a beefburger to reassure Muslim customers that there is no pork in it. Chicken restaurants of the Colonel Sanders type are common sights in urban shopping malls. Youngsters relish the freedom of a place not frequented by older folk. Office workers may choose to eat a pizza instead of going home for a home-cooked lunch.

McDonald's and Kentucky Fried Chicken outlets are decorated and managed like their prototypes in the United States, except that the language is, of course, Malay. Western fast food has become an attractive option among Malaysians, besides also being a comfortable retreat for Western tourists looking for the familiar meal of a burger, French fries, and Coca-Cola.

Fast food does not have to be foreign, though. Malaysians can get local food fast at canteen-style restaurants. There is no need to place an order and then wait for it to be cooked. Food here is cooked and ready. Each customer simply asks for a plate of rice and then chooses two to four side dishes from heated display trays. There is usually a wide variety of curries, vegetables, and fried foods such as fish, eggs, and peanuts to choose from.

Many rural secondary schools in Malaysia have boarding facilities. Food here is cooked in large quantities and often eaten in shifts, depending on the size of the mess hall. Each student gets a mound of rice with a few simple side dishes for flavor and nutrition.

INTERNET LINKS

www.malaysianfood.net

This website is dedicated to the culinary diversity of the multiethnic people of Malaysia with Malay, Indian, Eurasian, Chinese, and Nyonya recipes.

www.malaysianrecipes.co.uk

This is a free website with a wide range of Malaysian recipes, which are quick and easy to prepare, including noodles, curries, snacks, and classic favorites.

www.rasamalaysia.com

Rasa Malaysia is an Asian recipe and cooking website that includes many easy, authentic, and tested Malaysian recipes. Moreover this portal includes gorgeous food photography.

NASI LEMAK

This is Malaysian coconut milk rice served with spicy side dishes.

10.6 oz (300 g) long grain rice

⅛ teaspoon (0.625 ml) fenugreek (fennel) seeds

1 teaspoon (5 ml) salt

2 shallots

2 slices ginger, peeled

1.7 cups (400 ml) coconut milk

Rinse rice until clean. Place drained rice into a rice cooker together with shallots, ginger, fenugreek seeds, and salt. Pour in coconut milk to a depth of 0.8 inch (2 cm) over rice. Cook mixture until dry. Use a wooden spoon to loosen grains. Sprinkle remaining coconut milk over rice. Stir with a pair of chopsticks to distribute milk evenly. Leave to stand for 10 to 15 minutes. Keep warm.

Preparing the anchovy side dish

3½ oz (100 g) soaked anchovies

3 tablespoons (45 ml) oil

1 Bombay onion, sliced

2 tablespoons (30 ml) chili paste

1 thinly sliced stalk lemon grass

½ teaspoon (2.5 ml) chili granules

Seasoning

½ teaspoon (2.5 ml) anchovy granules

1 teaspoon (5 ml) sugar or to taste

2 tablespoons (30 ml) lime juice

2 tablespoons (30 ml) water

Pounded ingredients

5 shallots

2 cloves garlic

Ground ingredients

5 dried chilies, soaked

2 fresh red chilies, seeded

4 shallots

2 cloves garlic

¼ teaspoon (1.25 ml) chili granules

Juice of 2 large limes

Heat oil in a frying pan. Sauté pounded ingredients, chili paste, and chili granules until fragrant. Add anchovies and onions. Stir-fry well. Mix in lime juice, water, and seasoning ingredients. Mix well. Serve with rice.

Preparing the prawn side dish

10.6 oz (300 g) shelled medium-sized prawns

3 to 4 tablespoons (45 to 60 ml) oil

Seasoning

½ tablespoon (2.5 ml) sugar or to taste

½ teaspoon (2.5 ml) salt or to taste

¼ teaspoon (1.25 ml) chicken bouillon granules

Heat oil in a frying pan. Sauté ground ingredients until aromatic. Add prawns and cook for three to four minutes. Stir in lime juice and seasonings. Stir-fry well. Serve with rice.

SATAY CITARASA

10.6 oz (300 g) boneless beef
14 oz (400 g) squid
10.6 oz (300 g) chicken fillet
Bamboo skewers, soaked overnight
2 tablespoons (30 ml) oil

Ground spices

10 shallots
0.8 inches (2 cm) piece fresh turmeric
1.6 inches (4 cm) galangale
1.2 inches (3 cm) fresh ginger
½ teaspoon (2.5 ml) fennel seed
½ teaspoon (2.5 ml) coriander powder
1 tablespoon (15 ml) chili paste

Seasoning

2 tablespoons (30 ml) brown sugar
1 teaspoon (5 ml) salt or to taste
1 teaspoon (5 ml) soy sauce
3 tablespoons (45 ml) honey
2 tablespoons (30 ml) coconut milk

Cut the beef, squid (remove the ink bags), and chicken fillet into strips 0.8 inch (2 cm) long. Marinate the meat and squid with the ground spices and seasonings (reserve some for the glaze). Refrigerate, preferably overnight, and then add two tablespoons of oil to the marinated ingredients. Thread the meat and squid onto the skewers. Grill or barbecue the meat until dark brown.

Preparing the sauce

1 tablespoon (15 ml) fresh chili paste
2 tablespoons (30 ml) dried chili paste
8 shallots, minced
5 cloves garlic, ground
1 teaspoon (5 ml) chili granules
½ cup (125 ml) coconut milk
½ cup (125 ml) lime juice
3 tablespoons (45 ml) sugar
1 teaspoon (5 ml) salt or to taste
½ cup (125 ml) roasted peanuts, coarsely
  ground
1 stalk lemon grass, smashed
4 tablespoons (60 ml) oil

Heat the oil in a wok and fry the ingredients and lemon grass until aromatic. Add the coconut milk and lime juice. Bring to a gentle boil and simmer until the oil rises to the top. Stir in the ground peanuts, sugar, and salt. Serve with the grilled or barbequed meat.

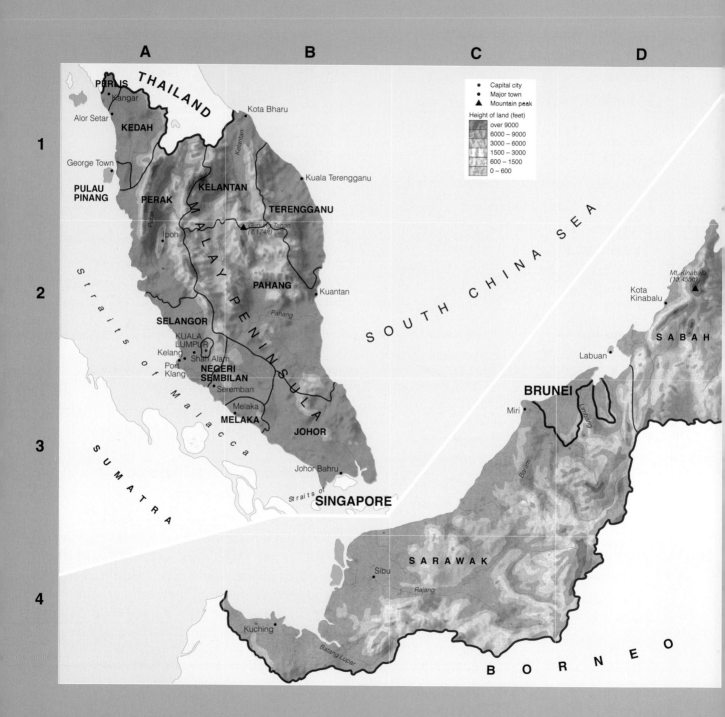

MAP OF MALAYSIA

E

N

Sulu Sea

Sandakan

Kinabatangan

Sulawesi Sea

Alor Setar, A1

Baram River, D3, D4
Batang Lupar River, C5
Bintulu, C4
Borneo, A5—F5, D4, E4, F4, E3, F3
Brunei, D3

George Town, A1
Gunung Tahan, B2

Ipoh, A2

Johor, B3, B4, C3, C4
Johor Bahru, C4

Kangar, A1
Kedah, A1
Kelang, A3
Kelantan, A2, B1, B2
Kelantan River, B1
Kinabatangan River, E3, F3
Kota Bharu, B1
Kota Kinabalu, E2
Kuala Lumpur, B3
Kuala Terengganu, B1
Kuantan, B2
Kuching, B5

Labuan, D3

Malay Peninsula, A1, A2, A3, B1, B2, B3, B4, C3, C4
Melaka, B3
Miri, D3
Mount Kinabalu, E2

Negeri Sembilan, B3

Pahang, A2, B2, B3
Pahang River, B3
Penang, A1
Perak, A1, A2, B1
Perak River, A2
Perlis, A1
Port Kelang, A3

Rajang River, C5, D5

Sabah, E2, E3, F2, F3
Sandakan, F2

Sarawak, B5, C4, C5, D3, D4, D5, E3, E4
Selangor, A2, A3, B2, B3
Seremban, B3
Shah Alam, A3
Sibu, C5
Singapore, C4
South China Sea, C2, C3, D2, D3
Straits of Melaka, A2, A3, B3, B4
Sulawesi Sea, F3, F4, F5
Sulu Sea, F1, F2
Sumatra (Indonesia), A3, A4, B4

Tawau, F3
Terengganu, B1, B2
Thailand, A1, B1

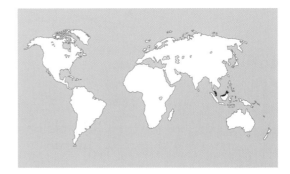

ECONOMIC MALAYSIA

Agriculture

🌴 Palm oil

🌳 Rubber

Services

✈ Airport

🚢 Port

🧳 Tourism

Natural Resources

🛢 Cement

🟫 Copper

⚓ Iron ore

⛽ Natural gas

🏭 Nitrogen

🛢 Petroleum refinery products

🪵 Timber

🛢 Tin

(Ti) Titanium

(TiO₂) Titanium dioxide

ABOUT THE ECONOMY

OVERVIEW

Malaysia's vision is to become a fully developed country by 2020. Today the country's economy is boosted by investments in high-technology industries, medical technology, and pharmaceuticals. Malaysia relies heavily on exports, especially of electronics, oil, and gas. The global financial crisis of 2008 severely affected worldwide demand for consumer goods, which in turn negatively affected Malaysia's economic growth in 2009. In 2010 the Tenth Malaysia Plan as well as a stimulus package worth RM67 billion (US$21.28 billion) was implemented by the government in an attempt to support the economy and to help country achieve its 2020 vision.

GROSS DOMESTIC PRODUCT (GDP)

$383.6 billion (2009 estimate)

GDP SECTORS

Services: 49.7 percent, industry: 40.9 percent, and agriculture: 9.4 percent

MINERAL RESOURCES

Tin, petroleum, copper, iron, natural gas, and bauxite

CURRENCY

US$1 = RM3.01 (June 2011)
1 ringgit (RM) = 100 sen

AGRICULTURAL PRODUCTS

Rubber, palm oil, rice, subsistence crops, timber, coconut, tropical fruits, fish, and pepper

WORKFORCE

11.38 million

EMPLOYMENT PROFILE

Industry 36 percent, services 51 percent, agriculture 13 percent

UNEMPLOYMENT RATE

3.7 percent (2009)

INFLATION RATE

0.6 percent (2009)

PORTS AND HARBORS

Bintulu, Port Klang, Kota Kinabalu, Kuantan, Kuching, Labuan, Melaka, Penang, Port Dickson, Sibu, Sandakan, Johor Baru, Tanjung Pelepas, and Tawau

MAJOR IMPORTS

Machinery, electronics, petroleum products, plastics, vehicles, chemicals, iron and steel products

MAJOR EXPORTS

Electronic equipment, liquefied natural gas and petroleum, palm oil, wood and wood products, rubber, chemicals, and textiles

TRADING PARTNERS

Singapore, Japan, Hong Kong, Thailand, China, South Korea, and the United States

CULTURAL MALAYSIA

George Town, Penang
Founded in 1786 by the British trader Francis Light, George Town is one of Malaysia's largest and busiest cities. The old part of the town is known for its well-preserved colonial buildings, with Chinese shop houses dating from the 19th century to the 1930s. Other interesting architecture includes Georgian civic buildings, Chinese mansions, Indian temples, and Acehnese mosques. The streets of George Town come alive daily with markets and hawkers. Places to visit include Fort Cornwallis and the Victoria Clock Memorial. George Town was inscribed a UNESCO World Heritage Site in 2008.

Kek Lok Si Temple, Penang
The largest Buddhist temple complex in Southeast Asia, the architecture is a mix of Chinese, Thai, and Burmese elements. Built around 1890, Kek Lok Si features a seven-tiered pagoda, also known as the pagoda of 10,000 Buddhas. An impressive 99-foot (30.2-m) bronze statue of the Kuan Yin can also be seen at the temple.

The Lenggong Valley
Known as the prehistoric capital of Malaysia, the Lenggong Valley is rich in prehistoric archaeological sites. It is situated in between the Titiwangsa and Bintang mountain ranges in Peninsular Malaysia. The area is believed to have been inhabited from as early as 1.83 million years ago covering the Paleolithic, Neolithic, and Metal ages. A wide variety of flora and fauna can be found in the Lenggong Valley.

Kinabalu Park, Sabah
Inscribed a UNESCO World Heritage Site in 2000, Kinabalu Park is dominated by the 13,435-foot-high (4,100-m–high) Mount Kinabalu. There exists a very wide range of habitats, from rich tropical lowland and hill rain forest to tropical mountain forest, even subalpine forest and scrub on the upper levels. Appointed a center of plant diversity for Southeast Asia, Kinabalu Park is rich in species with flora not just from Malaysia, but also from the Himalayas, China, and Australia.

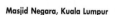

Masjid Negara, Kuala Lumpur
Built in 1965, Masjid Negara is the national mosque of Malaysia and an important symbol of the country's independence. It is also one of the largest mosques in Southeast Asia and can accommodate up to 15,000 people. The mosque's 240-foot-high (73-m-high) minaret contributes a striking structure to the city skyline. Another highlight of the mosque is its 18-pointed star-shaped central dome, representing the 13 states of the country and 5 central pillars of Islam.

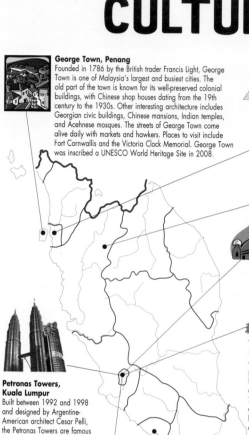

The Batu Caves, Kuala Lumpur
Situated 7 miles (13 km) north of the capital city, the Batu Caves are the sacred place for Malaysia's Hindu community. Discovered in 1892, these limestone caves can be reached by climbing a total of 272 steps. They consist of three main caves and a few smaller ones. The Hindu festival of Thaipusam is celebrated here.

Petronas Towers, Kuala Lumpur
Built between 1992 and 1998 and designed by Argentine-American architect Cesar Pelli, the Petronas Towers are famous for being the tallest twin buildings of the world. The pride of Malaysia, the towers reach a height of 1,482.9 feet (452 m) with 88 floors and 78 elevators. The impressive towers combine the best of high-tech modern engineering with the beauty of ancient Islamic design. The towers are connected by a skybridge on the 41st and 42nd floors, making it the highest two-story bridge in the world.

Gunung Mulu National Park, Sarawak
Inscribed a UNESCO World Heritage Site in 2000, this national park in northern Sarawak is significant both for its high biodiversity and for its tropical karst area. The 130,630-acres (52,864-ha) park contains 17 vegetation zones and 3,500 species of vascular plants. This vast park is dominated by Gunung Mulu, a 7,799-foot-high (2,377-m-high) sandstone pinnacle.

Niah Caves, Sarawak
Located near the city of Miri, these limestone caves, carved over millions of years, are home to millions of bats. The cave is an important prehistoric site where human remains, including a human skull dating to 40,000 years, have been discovered. Other prehistoric objects found include Pleistocene chopping tools and flakes, Neolithic axes, adzes, pottery, shell jewelry, boats, mats, then iron tools and ceramics and glass beads dating to the Iron Age.

Tun Abdul Razak Memorial, Kuala Lumpur
Built in 1961, the Tun Abdul Razak Memorial was established in loving memory of the second prime minister of Malaysia. The location of the memorial was the official residence of Tun Abdul Razak himself until his death in 1976. Tun Abdul Razak is remembered fondly by Malaysians for his sense of justice and his contribution to rural development.

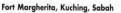

Fort Margherita, Kuching, Sabah
Built in 1879 Fort Margherita is situated in a commanding position along the Sarawak River. The fort was built as a defense against pirate attacks. Named after the second Rajah's Charles Brooke's wife Ranee Margaret, it was built in the defensive castle style of the late English renaissance. Today the fort is located within the police training barracks, and is home to the Police Museum, with its interesting display of Brooke militaria, weapons captured during the communist insurgency, and the famous "laughing skulls."

Melaka
Located on the West Coast of Peninsular Malaysia and founded in A.D. 1400, Melaka is an old city, which has preserved its rich cultural and architectural heritage. As a result of its strategic position as a center of the spice trade, Melaka was colonized by a host of rulers including the Dutch, Portuguese, and British. In 1989 Melaka was declared Malaysia's history city. Places to visit include the Baba Nyonya Heritage Museum, The Stadthuys (the official residence of Dutch Governors), and Bukit China (the official settlement of the Chinese entourage). Melaka was inscribed a UNESCO World Heritage Site in 2008.

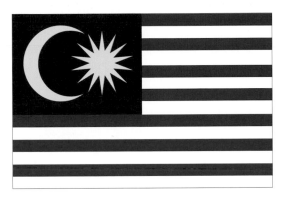

OFFICIAL NAME
Malaysia

CAPITAL
Kuala Lumpur

FLAG
Fourteen horizontal red (top) and white stripes (bottom) with a blue rectangle in the upper hoist-edge corner bearing a yellow crescent and 14-pointed star, traditional symbols of Islam.

NATIONAL ANTHEM
Negaraku (My Country)

POPULATION
28.3 million (2009 estimate)

LIFE EXPECTANCY
73.5 years

ETHNIC GROUPS
Malays: 53.3 percent, indigenous: 11.8 percent, Chinese: 26 percent, Indians: 7.7 percent, others: 1.2 percent

RELIGIONS
Islam (national), Buddhism, Hinduism, Taoism, Christianity, Sikhism. Shamanism is also practiced in East Malaysia.

LITERACY RATE
93.5 percent (2010 estimate)

LANGUAGES AND DIALECTS
Bahasa Malaysia (official language); English; Chinese dialects (Cantonese, Mandarin, Hokkien, Hakka); Tamil; Telugu; Malayalam; Punjabi; Thai. Indigenous languages, such as Iban and Kadazan, are also spoken in East Malaysia.

HOLIDAYS AND FESTIVALS
Fixed dates: New Year's Day (January 1), Labor Day (May 1), National Day (August 31), Christmas (December 25). Variable dates: Chinese New Year, Hari Raya Puasa, Hari Raya Haji, Good Friday, Easter, Wesak Day, Thaipusam, Deepavali

SYSTEM OF GOVERNMENT
Constitutional monarchy headed by a paramount ruler and a parliament consisting of a nonelected upper house and an elected lower house. Each state, except Melaka, Penang, Sabah, and Sarawak, has a hereditary ruler.

LEADERS IN POLITICS
Tunku Abdul Rahman (1957—70)
Dr. Mahathir bin Mohamad (1981—2003)
Mohamed Najib bin Abdul Razak (since April 3, 2009)

TIME LINE

IN MALAYSIA	IN THE WORLD

100 B.C.–A.D. 200
Emergence of trading kingdoms in the Isthmus of Kra.

1206–1368
Genghis Khan unifies the Mongols and starts conquest of the world. At its height, the Mongol Empire under Kublai Khan stretches from China to Persia and parts of Europe and Russia.

1776
U.S. Declaration of Independence

1789–99
The French Revolution

1914
World War I begins.

1939
World War II begins.

1941–45
The Japanese occupy Malaysia.

1945
The United States drops atomic bombs on Hiroshima and Nagasaki. World War II ends.

1946
Dato' Onn bin Ja'afar founds the United Malays National Organization (UMNO).

1948
The Federation of Malaya is formed.

1957
Malaya gains independence. Tunku Abdul Rahman becomes the first prime minister.

1965
Singapore leaves the Federation.

1967
Malaysia and Singapore establish the Association of Southeast Asian Nations (ASEAN).

1970
Tun Abdul Razak becomes prime minister. The New Economic Policy era begins.

1981
Mahathir bin Mohamad becomes prime minister and remains in office for 22 years.

IN MALAYSIA	IN THE WORLD
1997 Malaysia is hit by the Asian economic crisis.	**1997** Hong Kong is returned to China.
2001 Malaysia's worst ethnic clashes in decades between Malays and ethnic Indians	**2001** Terrorists crash planes into New York, Washington D.C., and Pennsylvania.
2003 Abdullah Ahmad Badawi becomes prime minister.	**2003** War in Iraq begins.
2004 Prime Minister Abdullah Badawi wins landslide general election victory.	**2004** Eleven Asia countries are hit by giant tsunami, killing at least 225,000 people.
2005 Acrid smoke, from forest fires on the Indonesian island of Sumatra, engulfs central areas and prompts a state of emergency.	**2005** Hurricane Katrina devastates the Gulf Coast of the United States.
	2008 Earthquake in Sichuan, China, kills 67,000 people.
2009 Badawi steps down as prime minister and is replaced by his deputy, Najib Abdul Razak.	**2009** Outbreak of flu virus H1N1 around the world
	2011 Twin earthquake and tsunami disasters strike northeast Japan, leaving over 14,000 dead and thousands more missing.

GLOSSARY

agong (ah-gong)
A king

amah (ah-mah)
A paid housemaid

ang pow (ahng-pow)
A small red paper envelope containing money given as a gift at birthdays, weddings, and the lunar New Year

Apa khaba? (ah-pah khah-bahr?)
How are you?

Aurea Chersonesus
Malaya's old name, meaning "peninsula of gold"

baju (bah-joo)
Clothing

batik
A fabric printed with colorful dyes

bumiputera (boo-MI-put-teh-RAH)
Native Malays; indigenous Malays

Hajj (hahj)
Muslim pilgrimage to Mecca

halal
Can be eaten by Muslims; halal food has no pork and is specially prepared

ikat (ee-kaht)
A uniquely patterned fabric woven by the Iban people of Sarawak

joss sticks
Incense sticks lighted by Buddhists when they pray

kampong
A village

kota (koh-tah)
A town or city

Orang Asli
Tribes living in the interior rural parts of Malaysia

orangutan
An intelligent red ape; literally "forest people"

pantun (pahn-toon)
Malay verse

puasa (poo-ah-sah)
To fast; Muslims eat nothing between breakfast and dinner during the month of Ramadan

Koran
Islam's holy book

songkok (sohng-koh)
A (usually) black cap worn by Muslim men to the mosque

FOR FURTHER INFORMATION

BOOKS

Cheam, Jeremy (editor). *Malaysia Insight Guide*. London: APA Publications, 2008.

Davis DiPiazza, Francesca. *Malaysia in Pictures* (Visual Geography). Minneapolis, MN: Lerner Publishing Group, 2006.

De Ledsema, C. et al. *The Rough Guide to Malaysia, Singapore and Brunei*, 6th ed. London: Rough Guides, 2009.

Emmons, R. *DK Eyewitness Travel Guide: Malaysia & Singapore*. London: Dorling Kindersley, 2008.

Munan, Heidi. *Malaysia (Culture Shock!): A survival guide to customs and etiquette*, 3rd ed. London: Marshall Cavendish, 2009.

Oon, Helen. *Globetrotter Travel Pack: Malaysia*, 7th rev. ed. London: New Holland Publishers, 2010.

Payne, Junaidi. *Wild Malaysia: The Wildlife and Scenery of Peninsular Malaysia, Sarawak and Sabah* (Wild Series), rev. ed. London: New Holland Publishers, 2007.

Richmond, Simon. *Malaysia Singapore and Brunei*, 11th ed. London: Lonely Planet Publications, 2010.

DVDs

Human Weapon: Silat: Martial Art of Malaysia. TravelVideoStore.com, 2010.

Travelview International: Malaysia. TravelVideoStore.com, 2009.

Vista Point: Kuala Lumpur, Malaysia. TravelVideoStore.com, 2005.

Weekend Explorer: Borneo, Malaysia. Barnstormer Productions, 2005.

Weekend Explorer: Kuala Lumpur, Malaysia. TravelVideoStore.com, 2005.

BIBLIOGRAPHY

BOOKS

Bird, I. *The Golden Chersonese: Travels in Malaysia in 1879*. London: Oxford University Press, 1980.

Major, John S. *The Land and People of Malaysia and Brunei*. New York: HarperCollins, 1991.

WEB SITES

About the Malaysian government. www.malaysia.gov.my/EN/Main/MsianGov/Pages/AboutMsianGov.aspx

Climate of Malaysia. www.malaysiatravel.org.uk/climate.html

Country profile—Malaysia. www.new-ag.info/country/profile.php?a=865

Kuala Lumpur climate. www.climatetemp.info/malaysia/kuala-lumpur

Malaysia energy data, statistics and analysis—Oil, gas, electricity, coal. www.eia.doe.gov/cabs/Malaysia/Full.html

Malaysia home page. www.geographia.com/malaysia

Malaysia: Education for all. www.unescobkk.org/fileadmin/user_upload/appeal/gender/MALAYSIAeducationforall.doc

Malaysia: Environmental health country profile. www.environment-health.asia/fileupload/malaysia_ehcp_07Oct2004.pdf

Malaysia: Environmental profile. http://rainforests.mongabay.com/20malaysia.htm

Malaysia—Construction industry news. www.export.by/en/?act=news&mode=view&id=19777

Malaysian environment statistics. www.nationmaster.com/country/my-malaysia/env-environment

Malaysian Rubber Export Promotion Council. www.mrepc.com/industry/

Mount Kinabalu. www.endemicguides.com/KinabaluNP2.htm

Niah National Park. www.forestry.sarawak.gov.my/forweb/np/np/niah.htm

Sahabat Alam Malaysia: The A—Z of the Malaysian Environment. www.suite101.com/lesson.cfm/17295/650/2

The Empowerment of Women. www.anugerahcsrmalaysia.org/2010/03/12/the-empowerment-of-women/

The World Factbook, Malaysia. www.cia.gov/library/publications/the-world-factbook/geos/my.html

Tin mining in Malaysia. www.mbendi.com/indy/ming/tinm/as/my/p0005.htm

Tin Mining. http://earthsci.org/mineral/mindep/depfile/tin.htmearthsci.org/mineral/mindep/depfile/tin.htm

Top ten longest bridge of the world. http://24-timepass.com/blogs/top-ten-longest-bridge-world.htm

United Nations Statistics Division—Demographics and Social Statistics, http://unstats.un.org/unsd/demographic/products/socind/hum-sets.htm

INDEX

INDEX